# A Literary Education:

## Adapting Charlotte Mason for Modern Secular Homeschooling

GW00481991

## By:

## Emily Cook

This book is dedicated to my mother, who made me a reader; and my children who taught me more than they will ever know and gave me an excuse to buy too many books.

# Table of Contents

# Forward

I've been homeschooling for a decade and a half, which seems insane to me. Sometimes I still feel like a newbie, and sometimes it feels like we've been homeschooling for an eternity – often in the same day. In that time, I've read my fair share of books about homeschooling, and something that I'm always looking for are practical examples. It's nice to read about different philosophies, but putting them into practice can be quite tricky, especially without any examples. So I made a concerted effort to include as many practical examples as I could within this text.

As I come to the end of my homeschooling career with my oldest, and the beginning of a new homeschooling journey with my youngest, I am continuously seeing what works and what doesn't, and I hope I can pass on some of that wisdom to all of you.

And finally, one of my reasons for writing this book is to bring the early 1900's Charlotte Mason's philosophy into the modern world. So much of the writing about her ideas, from books to blogs, feels old-fashioned, as if it were a snapshot of another time. I wanted to give voice to those who lean on her philosophy but still make use of modern novels, technology and more. I think that the two can live in harmony – one doesn't need to forsake all technology and modern entertainment in order to follow a literature-based lifestyle.

I hope that comes across in this book.

I like to think of this as a history of our homeschool. I hope you enjoy a peek into our life and our days.

# Introduction

For as long as I can remember, I have loved books. Going to the public library was one of my favorite activities growing up. My parents would take my brother and me to our undersized and understaffed county library, but I would bask in all the glorious books nonetheless. I loved to just walk through the bookshelves, touch the spines, and carefully choose the prettiest ones to bring home. I loved to flip through the pages, breathe in their smell, take in their tales of heroes and myths, castles, dragons and princesses in tall towers.

My parents didn't guide our book choices, they let us run free. That being said, I read a fair share of junk mixed in with some real literary gems. My mother loved to read, so I followed her example and read as much as I could. I spent much of my childhood holed up in my room, surrounded by piles of my favorite books, some of which, I read so many times they fell apart. I loved books, and when my husband and I started our family, I knew that I wanted to pass on my love of reading to my children.

Fast forward a few more years, and I was a young mom excited by the prospect of homeschooling my first daughter. I had just stumbled onto this wild idea when she was barely two years old. I had been dreading the idea of sending her off to preschool the following year, and came across an article on the internet about "home-preschooling". That article spoke to my heart, and I read and reread it several times. After contemplating my plan of attack, I excitedly pulled out a stack of picture books, crayons, paper, and alphabet blocks and away we went. We played, talked, drew pictures, sang songs, read tons of picture books, went for nature walks, baked cookies and cupcakes and just enjoyed life.

But when she turned 5, I had a moment of panic. Suddenly this whole homeschooling experiment was about to become a reality. People were expecting us to send her to public school, just like everyone else... after all, we also had twin toddler boys at home. How could I possibly be expected to educate my kindergartener while also dealing with the adorable chaos of twin toddlers underfoot?

So I did what any panicky new homeschooling mother would do. I purchased a random pre-packaged full kindergarten curriculum. I wanted to be official, and do it the "right way," so I could prove to the doubters that we were serious and we knew what we were doing. And if I had to show them a box, I could. See, official.

I was reflecting back upon my own public school education, and assumed that was the "be all end all" model that we needed to make sure we didn't miss anything important. I set up a little school area in a corner of our tiny apartment and we started our first day. My little girl happily played along. We went through all of our subjects – math, handwriting, phonics and reading; it went swimmingly. But a few weeks into this new, tedious way of doing things, we were both bored out of our gourds. We soldiered on and plugged away for nearly half the year before I threw in the towel in despair. This was not the way I had imagined things.

I sat down and thought about what had worked before the big box, and that's when I realized – we were hardly reading any real books. We were filling in endless workbook pages, and reading boring early readers. Busy work had taken over our days. By the end of the afternoon, we both needed a break. That's not what education should be, it shouldn't drain us of our energies. Real education should make you feel rejuvenated. Something was definitely wrong here, and we had only completed the first half of Kindergarten! I knew we needed to do something before we burned out or quit. Public school was just a few short blocks away...

That was when I went into research mode on the internet and discovered Charlotte Mason and her philosophy of education. It was as though someone had opened a window into our stuffy school room and let a fresh breeze blow through. I excitedly read about living books, literary narration, copywork and short lessons, and my heart soared. This was what I had been looking for! We did a mid-year overhaul and spent our days once more immersed in the world of beautiful books.

We lived in an apartment in the city, so we couldn't do much in the way of nature walks anymore, but whenever we visited my husband's parents (usually once a week) we spent time exploring in their yard. I quickly realized that I would never be a Charlotte Mason purist, but that's OK. There aren't any homeschool police that were going to ticket me for not doing handicrafts or spending six hours a day out-of-doors.

Around the same time I picked up a copy of *The Well Trained Mind* at a local library book sale and discovered Classical Education. I read so many other books that year, we had a period that I like to look back on as "What if this is a better way?!" mania – where we tried out nearly every philosophy I could read about – from Montessori to Waldorf to Classical.

I took bits and pieces from each and became very eclectic, but at the heart of it all were those tenets of Charlotte Mason philosophy that had first spoken to me: living books, narration, copywork and dictation, nature study and short varied lessons. Everything I liked from the other methods was easy to adapt and would integrate inside the Charlotte Mason framework.

**But what is a living book?**

To me, a living book is a book that comes alive when you read it. It leaves a mark when you've finished reading and lives in your heart forever after.

That might seem like a lot to ask of a book. You might be thinking that it might limit your choices to have to search for a book that fits that definition. Thankfully, there are thousands upon thousands of living books to choose from! We are so lucky to live in an age with such a plethora of literature right at our finger tips.

One of the first things I read about when I discovered Charlotte Mason was that children should be surrounded by wonderful ideas. They should be immersed in fairy tales and stories of heroes and other such things for them to think about and ponder. So I strove to fill our little homeschool with books that would fit that purpose. That first year, our homeschool library consisted of just one small bookcase in my daughter's room. But I began collecting books with fervor. I spent hours in our local bookstore and library scouring the shelves for the very best in children's books. I researched book lists like it was my job (because it now was).

Today our home is brimming with literature – from Tomie de Paola's folk art style picture books to Shakespeare's elegantly written plays to Tolkien's meticulously built fantasy world to A.A. Milne's Hundred Acre Wood. I have shelves of science books and history books, poetry, art and geography, I've tried my hardest to hit all "subjects." But I always hold each book to the living-books-test:

- *Is it written by an author who knows their subject?*
- *Does it hold my attention?*
- *Does it bring the subject to life?*
- *Does the story live and breathe?*

If the answer is yes, that book earns itself a place on my shelves.

Living books can be the foundation for a beautiful and rich education. It will give your child a feast of ideas, heroes to emulate, a rich vocabulary and provide a wide and varied education. These books will bring delight to your child, filling their mind with the best of the best.

# Chapter 1 - The Charlotte Mason Method

*"I am, I can, I ought, I will."* ~ *Charlotte Mason*

If you've been homeschooling for any amount of time, chances are you've come across the name Charlotte Mason. She has made quite a name for herself in the modern homeschool movement, despite the fact she lived over a hundred years ago. Charlotte Mason (1842 – 1923) was a British educator who advocated the improvement of the quality of education for children.

She promoted the idea of a "liberal education for all" not just those of a certain social class. She established a training school for governesses, and is often looked upon as one of the pioneers of home education. She co-founded the Parents Education Union, which provided resources to parents teaching their children at home. She also wrote several books and a magazine to help other people to understand her revolutionary ideas on education.

If you've ever searched for Charlotte Mason inspired curriculum or information, you probably found a variety of resources that seem to be very old-fashioned and very religious. It is true that Ms. Mason herself was a Christian who lived during the Victorian era. But that doesn't mean that we have to teach as if we are still living in that time period! While it may appear that the Charlotte Mason method of home education is outdated and too religious for a secular homeschooler to touch, I strongly disagree. Even though many of her ideas were based on Victorian era Christian ideals, her core education methods can and should be used in a modern homeschool – whether religious or not.

---

*"Education is an atmosphere, a discipline, a life." ~ Charlotte Mason*

---

When I began homeschooling my eldest child several years ago, discovering Charlotte Mason's educational philosophy was a stroke of luck. I was immediately drawn to the idea of educating with living books, so now much of what I do is based on this foundation of teaching. But it's more than just reading beautiful literature; it's creating a rather unique atmosphere of learning that you won't find in your local public school system. Load your bookshelves with the best literature you can find. Hang beautiful, thought-provoking art work around your house. Watch history and science documentaries as well as good movies and television programs. Listen to beautiful music (which, of course, is open to interpretation). Filling my home with beauty and grand ideas is one of the best ways that I have found to inspire my children with the best ideas the world can offer. And you can too.

> *"The question is not, — how much does the youth know? When he has finished his education — but how much does he care? And about how many orders of things does he care? In fact, how large is the room in which he finds his feet set? And, therefore, how full is the life he has before him?"* ~ *Charlotte Mason*

There are many basic tenants of the Charlotte Mason method of education that I feel you should try to incorporate into your daily homeschool routine. I am just going to give you an overview in this chapter. In later chapters I will go into more depth on these topics.

## Living Books

Literature is the foundation of the Charlotte Mason philosophy of education. Rather than studying from dry, formal textbooks, your children will be immersed in lovely prose and vivid writings from authors who care deeply about their subject matter. A living book is one that evokes emotion and draws you deeply into the story. Living books offer much for thoughtful contemplation, not just simply providing information to the reader.

The majority of Charlotte Mason websites, books, and curricula available on the market today focus on Victorian era literature. I imagine the thinking behind this is that they want to make their Charlotte Mason experience more authentic by only using what she herself would have used in her schools. While those books are quite lovely and can be valuable resources, there have been literally thousands of books written since 1923 that beg to be explored and appreciated. These wonderful books are absolutely just as worthy of your and your child's time. A few suggestions such as *The Evolution of Calpurnia Tate* (2009) by Jacqueline Kelly, *One Crazy Summer* (2010) by Rita Williams-Garcia, *Phineas Gage: A Gruesome but True Story About Brain Science* (2002) by John Fleischman, and *George vs. George: The American Revolution as Seen from Both Sides* (2004) by Rosalyn Schanzer are not to be missed. Were Ms. Mason alive today, surely these are the books she would be recommending to her teachers and parents.

Living books can appeal to all ages – they aren't childish and they don't have to be compartmentalized by grade level. You can read them aloud to your whole family, and everyone will get something from them. In a Charlotte Mason style homeschool, replacing your uninspiring textbooks with fascinating and well written literature and non-fiction will bring your studies to life.

## Copywork and Dictation

*"Perfect Accomplishment.-- I can only offer a few hints on the teaching of writing, though much might be said. First, let the child accomplish something perfectly in every lesson--a stroke, a pothook, a letter. Let the writing lesson be short; it should not last more than five or ten minutes. Ease in writing comes by practice; but that must be secured later."* ~ Charlotte Mason

Copywork and dictation form the backbone of the language arts in the Charlotte Mason method. In the beginning, copywork doubles as handwriting practice, and focuses on the neat and careful handwriting of single letters, then words and finally sentences. Once your child is comfortably writing full sentences, choose beautiful passages from the literature you are reading for them to copy. This is "killing two birds with one stone," in that you are working on their best penmanship, but also filling your child's thoughts with grand ideas and exposing them to examples of good writing.

Consider this method as learning to become a good writer by osmosis. If your children are immersed in a world full of living books and lovely thoughts, they will learn what good writing looks like and therefore, learn to write well.

When students become proficient at writing, you can begin dictation. Typically, it is begun around the age of 10, however, it can be begun earlier if your child is comfortable with writing. Dictation is similar to copywork, in that you will still choose beautiful passages of literature. But the difference is that instead of just copying the words in front of them, you will read the passage aloud for them to transcribe. This gives them the opportunity to take those passages of good literature and work on learning the mechanics of writing, such as end punctuation, grammar, spelling, and where to place the commas. This cultivates the essential skills of observation (they must study the passage first), listening, comprehension skills, and learning proper sentence structure.

## Narration

Narration is the basis for composition in a Charlotte Mason style homeschool. It takes the place of reading comprehension quizzes, inane discussion questions and tedious book reports. Narration is simply retelling, in their own words, what they have read or heard. Children naturally want to tell us about things they saw, heard or watched, so narration is a natural extension of that.

Ask your child to tell you what they remember after a reading. By telling it back to you, they will recall more clearly and for a longer period of time. It is essentially an oral composition exercise. They will have to focus their attention on the reading, then organize their thoughts and learn to express themselves clearly and coherently. To keep it interesting, narration can also take the form of creative assignments, such as creating a skit, a piece of art, or a short story – all based on the reading.

Once your child gets older and has been narrating orally for a while, you can begin written narrations. The method is essentially the same, but now they put their thoughts into writing. Again, to keep it interesting and not merely writing a summary of the reading every time – they can create a character journal, write a letter to the author, conduct an interview with a character, all while developing the skills of literary analysis. Coach them early on, and watch as they naturally pickup better writing skills on their own.

## Nature Study

*"This is all play to the children, but the mother is doing invaluable work; she is training their powers of observation and expression, increasing their vocabulary and their range of ideas by giving them the name and the uses of an object at the right moment,–when they ask, 'What is it?' and 'What is it for?'"* ~ Charlotte Mason

In Charlotte Mason's day, nature study was important facet of science study. In Victorian times, there wasn't much of a need for the average student to deeply study science. But it was very necessary to grasp a basic understanding about the immediate world around them such as local flora and fauna. To them, keeping a nature journal was more than just a scientific study, but a piece of artwork with beautiful plants and animals hand-drawn or painted in great detail.

In our modern world, it can feel like nature study is unnecessary. Why bother, when there are more important and interesting sciences to study? But nature study has many benefits that are too important to be overlooked. By getting outside and experiencing the natural world, your child will begin to develop observational skills, a keen sense of wonder, and a desire to deepen their scientific knowledge.

It may be easier to just stay indoors and watch a nature documentary on television, but our children also need the experience of seeing nature in the real world and become a part of it, owning the knowledge by collecting it themselves.

So how do you do it? You can get out once a week for a nature walk, learn the names of all of the plants in your neighborhood, go on a hike or walk along a nature trail once a month, visit a nature reserve or state park, choose a tree in your yard to study for a year, put out a feeder and observe the local birds, or choose a few insects to collect and study. Don't be afraid to get dirty! Get down on the ground and look at tracks, step into creeks and ponds to look more closely at the world beneath the water, lie on the ground to get a closer look at a line of ants. Nature study is all about careful observation, so look closely at the world around you and explore!

Two of my favorite resources for getting started with Nature Study are *The Nature Connection* (2010) by Clare Walker Leslie which is full of activities to get you outside, and *Nature Anatomy* (2015) by Julia Rothman, a beautiful book that will inspire your child to create their own nature art. Pair those with some field guides, a magnifying glass and a sketch book and you are ready to step into the out-of-doors.

## Short and Varied Lessons

At first mention, short lessons sound somewhat fishy to most people. Considering that most children spend upwards of 6 – 8 hours of their day in school then a couple additional hours working on homework – how can short lessons be a good thing? But the idea of short lessons is such an important aspect of Charlotte Mason's method, and if used correctly, it is an incredibly useful educational tool.

> *"You want the child to remember? Then secure his whole attention." ~ Charlotte Mason*

Short lessons allow you to keep your child's attention focused. If you remember back to those hour long lectures you would sit through in school – it was inevitable that your mind would wander and you would start to daydream about more interesting subject matter. Charlotte Mason suggested that a better way would be to spend a powerful 20 – 30 minutes engaging your child's mind. Rather than completing a page of 50 math problems, assign 10 and be sure your child can do them well. There is no meaningless busy work in this method of education.

Instead of watching the clock and spending an hour on math, an hour on history, and an hour on language arts – spend some time focusing your child's whole attention on those 10 math problems. When they are done, read a chapter from your history book and add something to your timeline or label a blank outline map. Then spend some time outside in nature. Upon coming indoors, you both go off to do some independent reading for 30 minutes. Ask them to tell you about what they read and have a meaningful discussion.

Short lessons discourage dawdling and encourage your child to give their best effort. Your formal lessons can be completed by noon, and the afternoons can be filled with errands, art, or just leisurely pursuing your passions.

## Handicrafts and Life Skills

When I first read about handicrafts, it felt superfluous to our homeschool. Basket weaving and knitting just felt so old fashioned. For years, I ignored anything to do with handicrafts. But after reading more about it I came to realize that what Charlotte Mason intended was for children to find worthwhile pursuits in their free time. Rather than just lounging around playing video games, we should encourage our children to find worthwhile and profitable pursuits. These do not need to be things like basket weaving. Many of them are life skills that we want to impart to our children – how to change a tire, mowing the lawn, and gardening, for a small sampling.

However, we also want to encourage our children to pursue creative pastimes. This is where you will follow their interests. Coding and game design can be worthwhile pursuits, as can playing a musical instrument, painting, sewing, and film-making. The idea is to guide our children in exploring activities that are meaningful in some way to their lives.

They can be something that lead to a career down the road, but they could also just become a hobby that makes them happy. Handicrafts should be useful in some way, which can be subjective. I would argue that music is necessary and useful, and your child might argue that filming skits or book reviews is useful. We want to give our children plenty of opportunity to explore hobbies and learn important skills that will be useful to them in adulthood.

*Our aim in education is to give a full life. We owe it to them to initiate an immense number of interests. Life should be all living, and not merely a tedious passing of time; not all doing or all feeling or all thinking - the strain would be too great - but, all living; that is to say, we should be in touch wherever we go, whatever we hear, whatever we see, with some manner of vital interest. ~ Charlotte Mason*

At first glance, Charlotte Mason's methods of education may appear old-fashioned and overly religious, a philosophy of her time period that shouldn't fit into our modern, technology driven world. It would be easy to dismiss, but if you examine the core of the method, it is still very worthwhile in a modern, secular homeschool with a little bit of adaptation. You don't need to follow her original dated reading lists, or even follow the method strictly in order to give your child the best possible education. Just fill their environment with beautiful and worthy ideas, spend time out of doors exploring the natural world and pursuing their passions.

Give your child a world full of heroes and myths, big thoughts to think about and things to fall in love with, ideas to ponder and inspire them. That is the best education possible – one in which they see learning as a life-long pursuit and not something that must be done within the "schooling hours" each day.

# Chapter 2 - What Makes a Book Living?

You often hear the words "living book" tossed around in homeschooling circles, but what constitutes a living book? Can it be subjective? What are spine books? Do we have to read only literature that was written over a hundred years ago? How can I use living books in my homeschool? In this chapter, I want to explore all of these ideas and discuss the nuts and bolts of educating our children with living books.

First, let's talk about the definition. A living book is well written. It is a book that draws you into the story, expands your imagination, causes you to care about the subject or characters and makes you think. A living book should enrich your life in some way, either by teaching you something or expanding your point-of-view.

Think back on your favorite books – the ones that truly stuck with you over the course of your life. Those are inevitably living books. They are the books that make it into our top ten lists, the ones with dog-eared pages and tattered covers that we read over and over again through the years. The books that become a part of us and we can't wait to share them with others. Books that become our friends.

Living books are written by an author who has a passion for what he or she is writing about. They have spent years immersed in their subject matter and you can tell by their prose that they are excited to share their passion with you. Now picture the opposite end of the spectrum – a committee or author who has been hired by a publisher to write on a pre-chosen topic. They may research their topic, but they give you just the facts, devoid of passion. The author of a living book is emotionally engaged in their subject matter, whether it is honey bees or volcanoes, and they bring that topic to life in a way that inspires your imagination.

Living books are often classics, but they aren't limited to them. While everyone can agree that the works of Twain, Shakespeare, Dickens, and Austen are worthy of study, there are many modern books, from writers like J.K. Rowling, E.L. Konigsburg, Philip Pullman, and Roald Dahl, that are just as worthy of our attention and often more relevant to our modern-day children. Living books can be any genre, from science fiction, to graphic novels, and even non-fiction. Beautiful writing and thought-provoking stories aren't limited to any one particular genre, so don't be afraid to explore new things!

There is a lot of debate, especially among purists, about how much of the current literature offerings should be given to our children. While I agree there is an unfortunate abundance of books that have been dumbed down for today's youth, there is still an abundance of quality literature being produced today. We should not be afraid of giving our children modern books to read. Along those same lines, just because a book was written a hundred years ago, doesn't automatically make it a living book. While I do want my children to build a rich vocabulary, sometimes the archaic phrasing and language in older books can take you out of the story. To me, a living book should engage your mind, not confuse it.

On the opposite side of the spectrum, we have "twaddle." Books in this category are those that talk down to a child, are badly written or overly predictable. Twaddle is the literary equivalent of eating junk food. For example, an over-long series of books, or books that are based upon popular children's television shows would be considered twaddle. They are often poorly written fluff, patronizing, and with very little or no substance whatsoever.

And like junk food, a little won't hurt you, but too much will make reading real literature more difficult. Too much twaddle can actually train your mind to be weak. Read nothing but these kinds of simple, poorly written books, and that's all you will ever be able to read. If you want to build up your child's brain, you must feed it beautiful ideas, rich and varied vocabulary, plot devices and characters that make you think and ponder what will happen next. These elements are rarely found in twaddle.

> *"For the children? They must grow up upon the best . . . There is never a time when they are unequal to worthy thoughts, well put; inspiring tales, well told. Let Blake's 'Songs of Innocence' represent their standard in poetry DeFoe and Stevenson, in prose; and we shall train a race of readers who will demand literature–that is, the fit and beautiful expression of inspiring ideas and pictures of life." ~ Charlotte Mason*

But what if a book that is deemed "twaddle" is your child's favorite book? Having defined the term, I must admit a controversial opinion. I dislike the word "twaddle" and I feel it is far overused in most

Charlotte Mason circles. While there are books that are absolute drivel, many books labeled as twaddle are just books that a particular person disliked. One man's twaddle is another man's treasure, right?

I had one child who devoured the entire Magic Tree House series when he was 6. These books would definitely fall under the definition of twaddle – more than 50 books in the series, very simply written, stilted dialogue, and quite predictable plots. However, he was a reluctant reader and was wary of making the leap from beginner books like Frog and Toad and Little Bear to chapter books. He loved being able to finish a book in a sitting, and chapter books intimidated him.

But the Magic Tree House series, with its short chapters and many illustrations genuinely helped him cross that bridge and get him to the next level. They also sparked his interest in a variety of topics, from Vikings to the Titanic. So while technically speaking, they fit the twaddle mold, they did hold merit for my child.

While some books are obvious twaddle (a picture book based on a popular cartoon character for example), others might be just what your child needs at that particular moment in time. No one should be book-shamed because what they are reading may not be something that Charlotte Mason herself would have chosen for her students. Even so, I have always refused to read aloud those kinds of books to my children. If they want to read twaddle in their free time, so be it. But if they want me to read to them, I will choose a better book.

Free reading time should be just that – free for the child to read whatever they want. But something that tends to happen when a child is served a steady diet of beautiful literature is that they lose their appetite for twaddle. Suddenly they'll notice the bad grammar or stilted dialogue, and they'll begin to choose better books all on their own.

With rare exception, textbooks are not considered to be living books – they do not breathe life into a subject. They are often written by committee, and while they can be useful for research purposes, they tend to be very dry and tedious to read. Textbooks tend to focus on surface level information – names, dates and definitions, without going very deeply into any one subject. Their purpose is to fill your head with facts so that you can recall them just long enough to pass a test. So while they are very good at their intended purpose, if you wish your children to develop a deeper interest in their studies, you will want to avoid them. Instead of textbooks, you'll want to use **spine books**.

What is a spine book? A spine book will form the backbone or "spine" of that particular subject. It's a book that you'll use over the course of a semester or the full school year, or even multiple years; and everything else within the subject will revolve around it. Living books aren't limited to fiction. Non-fiction can be written with great literary quality, covering a wide variety of topics – biographies about historical figures or scientists, subjects within science, history and geography. These books are written by one person with a passion for their subject matter. They bring the subject to life, or are beautifully illustrated, engaging your imagination and drawing you into the topic at hand. Rounded out with historical fiction or picture books, they will give you a much more satisfying education than the surface level knowledge most textbooks will imbue.

For example, if you are studying world history at the elementary level, my favorite spine book series is *Story of the World*. I know it can be a controversial choice, but read aloud by the parents, it is the most engaging book of history for that age level. I have read this series with all four of my children over the years, paired with the *Usborne Internet-linked World History Encyclopedia*. Round it out with plenty of great picture books and a few well-chosen historical fiction novels, and you have a complete history program.

When you base your child's education around living books, everything they learn becomes a richer experience. You peg important dates and events upon lively and well written stories, making them come alive. They might not remember the exact dates of the Civil War, but they'll remember the characters that they read about, the battles that were fought, and the leaders who struggled to bring an end to a terrible war. In the end, they gain far more than just a list of memorized names and dates. They gain real knowledge. This is true learning at its finest.

# Chapter 3 – The Importance of Reading Aloud

Reading aloud to your children is extremely important. I cannot stress that enough. It may be one of the most important things you do for them, educationally speaking. Most parents can find the time to read a picture book or two with their infants and toddlers, but once a child learns to read, that snuggly read aloud time usually ends. However, it is actually more important to continue that read aloud time, well into their school years.

**But my son (daughter) is fully capable of reading his own books. Why should I read aloud to him?**

There are so many fantastic reasons to continue reading with your child well beyond the preschool years! I am going to share my top 10 reasons to read aloud with your children:

**10.** Reading aloud creates a family bond, especially if there are siblings listening as well. Your children will fondly look back on their memories of listening to you read aloud, giggle over how you did "all the voices," and fondly recall favorites stories heard at your knee. Just because a book is considered "children's literature", doesn't mean it's childish. Many of my favorite books are written for children! A good story is a good story, and you will find that you enjoy many well-written books just as much (if not more) than your children. Some of my fondest memories are of reading aloud to my children. A few years ago, I read aloud *The Hobbit* (1937) by J.R.R. Tolkien with my twins, and my oldest daughter kept trying to listen in as she did her school work in the other room. I had read it aloud to her a few years before then, and it is still one of her all-time favorite stories. I can't wait until my youngest is old enough so I can help her discover Middle Earth and all of its charms.

**9.** Reading aloud will help to stimulate their imagination. When you read aloud, you don't have to choose books at any particular reading level. So while your child is just getting comfortable with simple beginner chapter books, you can read aloud books to them that are far above their actual reading level. You can expose them to fantasy worlds full of talking animals, knights and battles, distant countries... the literary world is wide open to you!

Literature is peopled with characters that your children will want to emulate and filled with places they'll want to pretend to go. Poetry will fill their minds with beautiful language and spark their own creativity with words and stories. They will create their own worlds and characters based on those that they hear you read about, imagining themselves into the story.

I have to share a favorite memory of my oldest daughter. When she was around 10 years old, we read *Journey to the Center of the Earth* (1864) by Jules Verne together in anticipation of the new movie being released. Around that same time, her bedroom door was broken and we had taken it off the hinges and set it against the wall. She had been playing quietly all afternoon when suddenly I heard a shout and a crash. I ran upstairs to see what had happened and my daughter was sitting under the door, which had tipped over and slammed into the dresser – creating a sort of cave. She had been pretend playing the story with her toys, and got a little carried away. She apologized and said she would never pretend Journey to the Center of the Earth again, because, as she put it, "That book is dangerous!"

**8.** Literature will expose them to difficult ideas and situations in a safe way. Life is full of hard truths, and what better way to learn of them than from a beautifully written story read to them by someone they love and trust? *Charlotte's Web* (1952) by E.B. White shows that sometimes, a beloved friend dies, not from any terrible illness or violent act, but simply because it is a part of life. Good literature will lead them to discover that bad guys aren't always dressed all in black, and good guys don't always do the right thing.

One of my favorite examples of this is the Harry Potter series by J.K. Rowling. Rowling introduces children to many grey characters. Severus Snape is a great example. When his background is revealed, my children were shocked – this person that they were sure was a villain was trying to do the right thing all along, albeit in the worst imaginable way. And Dumbledore, who is a leader among the 'good guys' put Harry into some terrifying situations without giving him nearly enough information beforehand. These characters are both shades of grey, which shows children that humans are not perfect, and even when we have the best intentions, we can still make mistakes.

Literature will also build empathy – they'll put themselves in the characters place, wondering how they would react in the same situation. How many times have you read a story and wondered if you would have done something different? When we read with our children, and discuss the character's actions and decisions, we can help them put themselves in someone else's shoes. This will help them to become more compassionate adults.

**7.** Reading aloud to your children will increase their vocabulary. Again, because you aren't limited to choosing books within their reading level, you can expose them to a world of beautiful language, much of it far beyond their reading level. And because you are reading it aloud, they'll know how to pronounce those difficult words. Children who hear good language use good language.

People were always amazed when my very young children would use words like "stupendous" or "delirious." They weren't young geniuses, I just read to them frequently, and I chose books above their reading level. This will also help build their thinking skills – rather than interrupt the story to ask about a particular word, they'll be more apt to use context clues to try and figure it out themselves. Listening to that beautiful language, they will begin to understand grammar and correct sentence structure. Paired with copywork and dictation, they'll have a better grasp on the English language than if they had spent years filling in endless grammar and vocabulary workbook pages.

**6.** Reading to your children, daily, starting when they are very young, will build their attention span. A child who's been read to his whole life will be able to concentrate and pay attention to something for far longer than a child who spends all of his time playing video games or watching television. Just 20 – 30 minutes of reading a day can make all the difference. A child who has been read to will have a sense of curiosity that is missing in many of today's book starved youth.

**5.** Reading interesting and beautiful books aloud to your child will go far to instill a love of reading. Children who are brought up amongst literature grow up to become readers. This might sound obvious, but if you strew books around your house that your children might be interested in reading, read to them daily, and overall make reading a pleasurable experience, then your children will likely come to enjoy reading. Also, lead by example! Let your children see you reading, especially Dad. Children are great imitators, so let them imitate your reading habits. I want my children to see that reading isn't just a "school" activity, but a life activity.

**4.** You are giving your child a world of cultural literacy. I can't even begin to tell you the number of times literary references come up in life – socially, in other media, within other books. By reading widely to my children, from poetry to fairy tales to science fiction, I am providing them with knowledge that will help them to understand all of those references that come up later in life. 42!

**3.** Not only will reading build their imagination and give them deeper cultural literacy, it will lead them to their passions. Your children will discover new ideas at your knee. After reading the book *The Tarantula in My Purse* (1996) by Jean Craighead George, one of my sons became fascinated by birds. He's spent many years birdwatching, reading about different bird species, and watching birding programs that come on television. He is our resident bird expert, and it all started with a mother reading a book aloud to her children. Reading to your children will spark learning and lead them to their passions – from history to birding to space.

It can also lead to raising the next generation of writers. When you read great literature with your children, you are showing them what quality writing looks and sounds like. You are developing their imagination muscles and teaching them how good stories work. My oldest daughter has been writing stories since she was 6, and at 17 she is planning on majoring in creative writing when she goes to college. Many of the early stories she wrote sounded similar to her favorite books. She wrote a story about a girl who traveled through time to Ancient Greece to fight with Jason and the Argonauts. She explored different types of story writing before settling on her favorite – fantasy. By imitating her favorite authors, she was developing her own writing skills. All of that stemmed directly from our special read aloud time together.

**2.** Reading aloud introduces your children to books they might have never chosen on their own. Most children tend to stick to what they know when looking for new books. They might only read fantasy, or only read realistic contemporary fiction. But when you choose books to read aloud, you can choose genres that they might never have heard of otherwise. There is a world of books out there – from science fiction, to dystopian literature, to classics they might have been afraid to try on their own, to mythology.

My oldest child fell in love with mythology after I read her *D'Aulaire's Greek Mythology* (1962). She has since read as much mythology as she could get her hands on – Egyptian, Greek, Chinese, Japanese. She eats it up. She's even written short stories based on myths that she particularly loved.

**1.** But most importantly – reading to your children will give them a love of literature. I mourn for the children who grow up thinking Winnie the Pooh is just a brightly colored cartoon character on TV and never got to meet Charlotte and Wilbur, Sara Crewe, Charlie Bucket, Samwise Gamgee, or Tom Sawyer.

Reading aloud will give them a respect for the written word, introduce them to the wide world and the great conversation and build their cultural literacy. It will give them a legacy of great literature to pass on to their own children.

## Well-read children become well-read adults.

They are more likely to be highly educated, good writers and communicators. They will be more likely to pick up a book as an adult, rather than flip on the television or play on their smart phone or tablet. This next generation of children are growing up in a time of amazing technology but are quickly becoming addicted to screens. They are everywhere and incredibly hard to ignore. Reading aloud to them now is a great way to counteract some of the technological "noise" and give them time to develop their own imaginations away from screens.

When I first began homeschooling, I fell in love with the idea of a book based education. I daydreamed about reading aloud beautiful literature to my serene children, as they snuggled close to me on the couch, their little eyes focused on me with rapt attention as I read. But the reality was something quite different.

I had always read to my children at bedtime, but it wasn't until I began homeschooling in earnest that I added in a daytime story session. At that time, my oldest was 4 and I had one-year-old twin boys. That quiet snuggling time only happened if I planned our reading sessions around their naps. Otherwise it was chaos.

Things plugged along pretty smoothly, and I got through a hefty stack of books with my daughter. I was patting myself on the back, thinking I had everything figured out, until the twins got older and gave up their afternoon nap. I suddenly had no quiet moment in my day where I could continue our peaceful reading time. I would attempt to include them, but they were physically incapable of sitting still for longer than 10 seconds and the both of them were SO LOUD and full of vigor. We went from reading a chapter book every other week to one each month, if we were lucky. I felt defeated by these little balls of energy. I began to question if it was worth the trouble to even try reading aloud anymore.

That was when I finally had my epiphany. As I contemplated the future of our little homeschool, I realized that if my end goal was to have well-read children who loved the written word and who loved to learn, then I had to find a way to prioritize reading aloud. *It was literally the most important thing I could do for them.*

Reading aloud has numerous benefits, as we've already discussed, but for me, at that time, the biggest was giving my children a love of reading. I wanted them to appreciate books, to see them as the ultimate form of entertainment as well as a place to seek knowledge. Reading is powerful, and I wanted to give them that power.

But in those early days, it was hard. How do I read aloud when they won't sit still? When they interrupt every other sentence to ask a question? When the constant barrage of questions doesn't even have anything to do with what we're reading? When they argue for 30 minutes over which spot on the couch is "their spot?" How was I supposed to create this environment where we could read great books and discuss them, and most importantly THINK about all of those beautiful ideas when it felt like I was sitting in the middle of a three-ring circus?

First – I needed to realize that at that point in time, we weren't going to be reading in solid hour long chunks. I set aside different times throughout the day that would be devoted to reading. I discovered that while they were sitting at the table eating, I could read for 15 minutes without anyone running around the room or arguing over where to sit.

So I read poetry over breakfast and a chapter from our read aloud at lunch. I would let them run around outside for an hour and tire them out, and then we'd snuggle on the couch with a stack of picture books. On rainy days when everyone was a bit wired, I'd give them paper and crayons and let them draw while I read. Or I'd make hot chocolate and cinnamon toast and we'd have a story time tea party.

Second, and I think this is nearly as important as reading aloud, I needed them to see me reading for pleasure as well as for educational purposes. I touched on this above, but I think it bears repeating. Mothering is all about imitation, and I wanted them to imitate my love of reading. If they see that I'm always on the computer checking Facebook or grabbing my phone to "just check in for a minute" all day long, they will actually learn to value time wasted on the internet.

But if they see me spending my free moments reading a book, researching for our spring garden, or studying a topic that interests me, they'll learn that reading is a pastime worth pursuing. It's music to my ears when my children come to me with a question and then ask if we can go to the library to find a book about it. Or when my daughter comes running down the stairs clutching a book to her chest and telling me, "you HAVE to read this book, Mama!" That's when I know that I'm on the right path.

Difficulties come up along the way, but if you keep your focus on the end goal, and simplify your day when necessary, the important things can and will get done. School can consist of reading beautiful books and talking about the big ideas contained within. It honestly is enough.

Literature *can* be the focus of your studies. You may never experience that daydream scenario, with the billowing white curtains and the calm, serene children sitting silently while you read for hours. In fact, some days it will be incredibly hard. But in the end, you will give them the most important gift – the gift of literature, a thirst for knowledge, and most importantly, the love of learning.

# Chapter 4 - Reading Aloud: Making it Happen

By now, you are hopefully convinced that this reading aloud business is something you want to add into your day. But how? We're all busy, and let's face it, while you agree that it's important, it feels like just another chore to add to your never-ending daily to do list. In this chapter, I'm going to talk about the mechanics of reading aloud, and how to ensure that you can make the space to fit it into your day.

So you've chosen a topic to study and you've gathered your books. What exactly does teaching with literature look like? How can you fit all of that reading aloud into your day? It might appear to be a lot of work for the parent, and it is. I'm not going to lie, there is no way around it: This is not hands-off homeschooling. You will have to commit to reading with your children and discussing what you have read. But it doesn't have to be difficult. There is a method to the madness.

I spend the bulk of our homeschool day reading with my children. We are immersed in literature as a family and it has become our lifestyle. I break it up throughout the day, but I probably spend a good 3 hours each day reading with my kids. In this way I can introduce literature that they may not choose on their own – whether it's classics like *Tom Sawyer*

(1876) by Mark Twain or contemporary dystopian young adult literature like *The Hunger Games* (2008) by Suzanne Collins. I read aloud their history and science lessons so that we can discuss them together as we read, and I try to read poetry aloud a few times a week. Once a year we even manage to fit in a Shakespeare play. We have a beautiful rhythm of reading to shape our days.

It can be tricky to figure out how to fit in all of that reading in a typical day. Sometimes the day just gets away from you and suddenly it's bedtime and you realized you didn't read aloud at all. It took me awhile to figure out how to make it work. Years ago, I read on a Charlotte Mason message board this idea about pegs – pegging things that you want to make happen onto events that always happen.

For example – you're going to eat meals together at least twice a day, every day. So peg a reading session to a meal – poetry with breakfast, or history at lunch. You could peg your current read aloud novel to bedtime. It doesn't have to be one huge chunk of reading – if you tried that you would likely go hoarse! Breaking it up over the course of the day not only makes it more doable, it keeps everyone's mind fresh and attention focused.

It is difficult, I've found, for some children to sit still and stay focused for more than 20 - 30 minutes at a time. They start to fidget, their minds wander and before you know it, they haven't heard a single word you've said. Spreading out your readings ensures that they are able to focus on their lessons. It's another one of Charlotte Mason's wonderful ideas - short lessons help children to keep their focus. When you're reading aloud it's so important for them to be able to give their full attention.

We don't want to make it difficult by droning on and on for hours. No one wants to become the Ben Stein character from Ferris Beuller! I try to keep a reading session to no more than 30 minutes, unless they are truly engaged and ask me to read longer. We once read about 4 long chapters of *Harry Potter and the Deathly Hallows* (2007) in a sitting - we read the whole book, nearly 800 pages, in a little less than 2 weeks, because they just had to know how it was going to end!

Even so, sometimes it can be difficult, especially if this is something new to your family, to get your child to sit still and listen to a whole chapter, even a short one. Some tips I can give you is to start reading aloud after a session of outside time - let them run around the yard, jump on the trampoline, take a nature walk, do something that might tire them out a bit so that they aren't quite as antsy during reading time. Another thing that I find helps with my children is to let them draw while they listen. They can draw whatever they like, it doesn't have to have anything to do with what we're reading, but it keeps their hands busy and their minds focused. An alternative to that is playing with clay or silly putty, anything to keep those hands busy and their mind focused on the story.

And what about the babies and toddlers? It's certainly not easy, but still completely doable. When my youngest was a baby, I made sure she took at least one good nap each day and we squeezed a lot of reading time in with her siblings during her nap. When she stopped napping, I gave her crayons and paper to draw, or we got out the Play-doh or blocks and she played while we read. Having a special basket of "reading-time-only" toys can be a lifesaver. And she gleaned a lot from those readings! Sometimes I'd hear her talk about Harry Potter or Bilbo while she was playing with her toys. She may not remember much about the plot, but she was definitely still listening.

I love the idea that she and her siblings are growing up within a culture of reading. And of course I read aloud to her books at her level as well. She gets her own special time where we can sit and read picture books, some that I have chosen and some that she chooses off of the shelf. Start them young! A child who grows up with reading will grow up to be a reader. There are so many fantastic quality picture books to enjoy with your babies and toddlers. Board books aren't just for chewing. I always kept a small basket with board books within my toddler's reach so that they could easily choose one for us to read together.

When my oldest was small, she had a small handful of favorites that we read every day. One day I went in to get her up from a nap and heard her talking – when I peeked into the room she was sitting up in bed with her doll in her lap "reading" a book to her from memory. It was the sweetest thing to see her playing mother by reading to her baby.

Sometimes I will choose a read aloud that I think the whole family will enjoy so that I can include everyone in the experience. Everyone got into the *Harry Potter* series and *The Hobbit*. From the youngest (who was just 4 at the time, but still runs around trying to stun her siblings with a wand while riding around on her child sized broom) to the oldest.

There might be difficulties adjusting to this new lifestyle for mother as well. If you aren't used to reading aloud, it can be a challenge to go from a picture book or two at bedtime to reading for 2 – 3 hours of your day. Make friends with throat drops and drink plenty of water. This will help keep you from losing your voice. Another tip, and this will sound odd, but be sure you are sitting with good posture. If you are slouching then it is likely that you aren't breathing properly; therefore your voice will not hold out for a very long reading session. I find that propping a pillow behind my back can help me sit straighter.

Also, remember to ease yourself into it. Don't try to read a meaty history text, a difficult work of literature, a biography about a scientist, and poetry all at once. You'll burn yourself out before you start!

Instead, start with an easy, short chapter book like *The Courage of Sarah Noble* (1954) by Alice Dalgliesh or *My Father's Dragon* (1948) by Ruth Stiles Gannett, then add in a fun poetry book - I love Shel Silverstein's works: *A Light in the Attic* (1981) or *Where the Sidewalk*

*Ends* (1974), or other beginning poetry. Once everyone is used to the idea of reading aloud, you can start adding in more.

If you are starting with older children, you won't have to read aloud nearly as much. Around the age of 12, I start handing off some of the reading responsibility to my children. They've been reading on their own for many years at this point, and their comprehension is strong enough that they can take ownership of the history and science readings. We still read literature and poetry together, but they begin to take on some of the work of reading their lessons.

If you are jumping into a literature-based lifestyle with a tween or teen, it might take some adjusting. They might even scoff at the idea. But don't throw in the towel just yet. Choose an engaging and fun book to share – one of our family favorites is *The Hitchhiker's Guide to the Galaxy* (1979) by Douglas Adams. Even the most reluctant listener will come around to a hilarious romp through space. Serve them a treat, some hot chocolate and cookies, make it an event. Maybe they'd rather take turns reading.

You might also find they appreciate (and get more out of a story) if you watch the movie after you finish reading the book to compare the similarities and differences. So many fantastic pieces of literature have one or several movie adaptations. I have found it is a great way to discuss story structure, character development, and more by watching a movie adaptation after finishing a novel with my teens. We talk about why storylines were dropped, how they altered favorite scenes, added or eliminated characters – it's a great tool to help a reluctant child engage in a story. Find what works best for you and your children.

Another thing to help you ease into this transition to a more literary lifestyle is to make it fun for you and your children. I have always considered myself a bit of a theatric. I love to really dig into the story and live there for a while. I do voices for as many characters as possible, I read with emotion and act out the story for my children. And if I get a little emotional, that is OK. They are used to seeing me cry and sob my way through the end of a story.

I was a mess for the last several chapters of *The Book Thief* (2005) by Markus Zusak, a novel about one girl's experiences living in Germany during World War II, but I am so happy that I was able to share that reading experience with them. If you aren't used to it, that's OK - start small and play around with different accents. Try reading with lots of emotion - if a character is upset, let your voice show it. This truly goes a long way to bringing a story to life and making read aloud time an exciting and fun experience for everyone.

Try to choose books that you are familiar with so that you are comfortable taking on the roles of the different characters. One of the first chapter books I ever read aloud to my oldest daughter was *A Little Princess* (1905) Frances Hodgson Burnett. I still had my beloved copy that I had read over and over as a little girl, and I was so excited to share it with her. Because it was already one of my favorite stories, it made it incredibly easy to jump into the role of Sara Crewe, and convey the emotions of losing her father, losing her place in Miss Minchin's school, and adjusting to a life of poverty.

Becoming the villain was equally as fun. Bringing those characters to life that had lived and breathed in my imagination for so much of my childhood, was one of my favorite experiences in our early homeschooling days. It made me love the book so much more when I could share it with my child.

Remember that it isn't just about reading and letting your children tell back what they heard. Discussion is a crucial factor in reading aloud. After having my children narrate, we'll talk about things that I got from the story. We talk about terms like protagonist and antagonist, why the author chose a setting and what might be different if the story were set elsewhere, and how we might relate to a character. If your child has a tough time talking about the book at first, ask them open ended questions. Even just saying, "What would you do in their shoes?" is enough to spur on a discussion. Talk about what you think the author is trying to tell you with the story. What is the conflict? How do you think the conflict will be resolved? This is the beginning of literary analysis. Guiding our children through analysis while they are young will make it that much easier for them when they are dissecting Dickens and Tolstoy in high school or college.

I once heard someone say that you can always make time for what is important to you. Though there are days when it seems impossible, if reading aloud to your child is your goal then you can find a way to make it happen. Reading aloud can and should be the best part of your day. It is a legacy that you will leave behind for your children. My oldest is already planning out which books she's going to be permanently borrowing from our family library to relocate to hers when she starts her own family so that she can read them to her own children. To me, that's worth more than gold.

# Chapter 5 - Teaching Academics with Literature

So often I hear kids (and even adults!) say that history is boring. Or they think math is tedious, or science is dull. These are all fascinating subjects that help us to understand the world in which we live. How could they ever be boring? But they are so often taught with tiresome textbooks with a focus on memorizing names and dates, and formulas and vocabulary, which completely misses the point of learning.

> *I think we owe it to children to let them dig their knowledge, of whatever subject, for themselves out of the "fit" book; and this for two reasons: What a child digs for is his own possession; what is poured into his ear, like the idle song of a pleasant singer, floats out as lightly as it came in, and is rarely assimilated. I do not mean to say that the lecture and the oral lesson are without their uses; but these uses are, to give impulse and to order knowledge; and not to convey knowledge... ~ Charlotte Mason*

Well, luckily for you, any school subject can be taught with living books! Science, history, art, grammar, even math can be taught with lively and lovely literature! Most homeschoolers are familiar enough with how to liven up their history and science lessons with living books, but living books can breathe life into *any* subject.

We live at a time when there is an abundance of print. There are more books than we could ever even fathom being able to read in our lifetime. With the advent of e-books and e-readers, entire libraries of literature have become accessible whenever we wish from almost anywhere! Rather than finding ways of fitting good literature in around your homeschool curriculum, living books can BE your curriculum.

Living books are the tools by which your children can gain an amazing and thorough education. They can teach the basics of proper English grammar, spelling and vocabulary, guide us through the grand scope of history, explore different countries, and help us to learn empathy by experiencing life through someone else's eyes. They can help us to understand scientific concepts, critical thinking and so much more.

Let's go subject by subject and explore ways to add in a living books element to your studies.

# History and Geography

History and geography are the easiest to implement in a literature-based homeschool curriculum. There are thousands upon thousands of living books to choose from to round out your studies.

First, you'll want to choose a solid spine book for the foundation of your history studies. What is a spine book you ask? A spine book is one which serves as the foundation, or backbone, of your studies. This is a book you will build the rest of your course of study around. It doesn't, however, need to be a textbook. There are a plethora of well written, engaging books that can serve as a spine.

I like *The Story of the World* series by Susan Wise Bauer, as well as the *A History of US* and *The Story of Science* series, both by Joy Hakim. These books are all very well written and engaging, which is precisely what you'd want in a subject spine. Once you have chosen your spine, you'll need to choose some literature to round out your history studies. Your spine will give you a solid foundation with which to build the rest of your history studies upon. It will keep you on track as you cover a large scope of history, ensuring that you don't miss any important historical events.

A caveat: you don't need to cover every single topic in depth. Some topics you can just touch on briefly, while others lend themselves more easily to going down a rabbit trail. You'll know, as you are reading the spine together and discussing what you read, which topics you and your child will want to spend more time studying. Choose just a few topics to explore and to dig into.

I love historical fiction, but one can easily get carried away – there is just so much of it and it's very easy to overdo. While some stories are true to history, like *Johnny Tremain* (1943) by Esther Hoskins Forbes, *Fever 1793* (2000) by Laurie Halse Anderson, and *Girl in a Cage* (2002) by Jane Yolen, you need to be careful with inaccurate historical fiction. When well written, they *could* potentially lead to a research project to determine the actual truth. But these works can just as often cause confusion, especially with younger children.

It's wise to balance out all that historical fiction with some well written non-fiction, like Diane Stanley's beautifully illustrated biographies, or anything by

Russell Freedman, like *Lincoln: A Photobiography* (1987) or *Immigrant Kids* (1980). Having a good mix of well researched historical fiction and well-written non-fiction titles can bring your history studies to life and help your child to have a deeper understanding of that time. Just be careful not to overdo it. A few well-chosen books are plenty.

Add in a timeline, some well-chosen documentaries and movies, a writing assignment or project, and a field trip or two (when possible), and you have an excellent history curriculum built around living books.

There are different points-of-view to keep in mind about how to study history – do you want to go chronologically or hop around by interest? Four year cycle? Six year cycle? There are so many different ways to go about it, and in the end, all of them are right. The best choice is the one that makes the most sense to you. Charlotte Mason ideology states that chronological is best, but as I said, I am by no means a purist. I am a big believer in doing what works best for your child.

This is one area where I think people tend to stress themselves out unnecessarily. As long as you provide your child with the tools to learn on their own - teach them to read well, to express themselves, and to find the answers to their questions - they'll be able to make up for any gaps in their learning later on. We all have learning gaps - it is inevitable. Missing out on learning about the Crusades or Lewis and Clark and Westward Expansion won't harm their ability to get into a good college or their ability to function as a successful adult.

Geography is another subject that easily lends itself to studying with living books. Choose a place to learn about and then find the best books on the market about what it is like to live there. For instance, if you want to learn about Russia, you absolutely must read *Sovietrek: A Journey by Bicycle Across Russia* by Dan Buettner (1994), which is sadly out of print but well worth the effort of tracking down. The author and a few friends bike across the entire country, and he talks extensively about the land, the people he meets, the way they live, the food they eat, as well as the mechanics of going on such a massive biking expedition. It is a fascinating book filled with full color pictures and it makes a perfect spine for studying this fascinating country.

Once you have found a spine it is time to flesh it out a bit with some historical fiction like *Breaking Stalin's Nose* (2011) by Eugene Yelchin (a story about a boy living during the frightening days of Stalin's reign over Russia) or *The Night Journey* (1981) by Kathryn Lasky (one of my all-time favorite books about a Russian Jewish family fleeing the pogroms of the early 1900s) or *Angel on the Square* (2001) by Gloria Whelan (a story about a noble girl living through the Russian revolution as she witnesses the fall of the Romanov family and Tsarist Russia). Add in some Russian fairy tales like *The Tale of the Firebird* (2002) by Gennady Spirin and *The Magic Nesting Doll* (2000) by Jacqueline K. Ogburn, try out a few recipes for traditional Russian cuisine, learn about the native animals and ecosystems, and you are well on your way to immersing yourself and your children in Russia and Russian culture without even having to leave your house!

One of my favorite units that my children and I studied was a Russia unit. In addition to reading the literature I have recommended above, we also created a huge poster-sized map of Russia to label. We marked the places mentioned in the books we read, the path the bikers took in Sovietrek, and any major landmark we read about. My children drew animals and pasted them into the correct parts of the country where they might be found, and colored the map in sections to show where each ecosystem was located. We cooked Russian food, and painted our own set of Matroyshka dolls (that I still have decorating a shelf in my living room). They learned a great deal of information, and because we learned it in a fun and interesting way, they retained what they learned.

The best part about this method, is that rather than just knowing a few surface facts about Russia – the capital, population, language spoken, etc., you will learn about the country deeply – you'll find out what it is like to live there, the kinds of foods typically eaten, what the people who live there believe, how they behave, etc. Your children will experience what it is like to be Russian, all while still at home, comfortably and safely at your side. If you have a family ancestral tie to a particular geographic area, deep diving into those particular countries will give your children a greater understanding of the lifestyle and hardships of great-grandparents or other distant relatives.

# Science

Studying science with literature works similarly to the way you study history. Choose a spine based on the topic you want to study – there are so many fantastic science encyclopedias on the market today that can serve nicely as a spine. I like these because they tend to have a lot of great photography and illustrations that are dying to be drawn and labeled. They aren't necessarily the most literary choices, but that is ok. We're going to round them out with more literary fare. My personal favorites are the *Kingfisher Science Encyclopedia* (2011) the *DK Encyclopedia of Science* (2006) and the *Usborne Internet-linked Science Encyclopedia* (2003). Armed with any one of these beautifully illustrated books, you can then round out your study with biographies about scientists, such as *On a Beam of Light: A Story of Albert Einstein* (2013) by Jennifer Berne, or *Radioactive: A Tale of Love and Fallout* (2010) by Lauren Redniss.

Choose a topic that your child is especially interested in and ask your local librarian to help you find a stack of books on that topic. There are so many wonderful children's science books on the market! Interested in brain science? Check out *Phineas Gage: A Gruesome Yet True Story About Brain Science* (2002) by John

Fleishman, a true account about a man who had an iron rod shot through his head and lived to tell the tale. Do you want to get out and explore nature? Read *One Small Square: Backyard* (1997) by Donald Silver.

Non-fiction doesn't have to be boring. If you have a teen, there are some amazing literary resources. Studying chemistry? You should read The *Disappearing Spoon: And Other True Tales of Madness, Love, and the History of the World From the Periodic Table of the Elements* (2010) by Sam Kean. Bill Bryson's *A Short History of Nearly Everything* (2003) makes a fantastic spine for a high school level general science course. He covers a huge range of scientific concepts and he makes them all sound so interesting that you'll want to research and learn more. I have found that even the most reluctant science student can be reeled in with a well written book.

Reading a variety of fascinating books on a scientific concept will be a much more in-depth study of the subject than would be had by reading a chapter in a dull textbook and answering a few meaningless comprehension questions.

Not all science books are non-fiction. My children adored the Magic School Bus series of picture books when they were young, and you can have quite a solid science curriculum just based around those books and videos. While studying chemistry with your middle grade student, you might want to read *Itch: The Explosive Adventures of an Element Hunter* (2014) by Simon Mayo, a series about a boy named Itch who collects specimens of every element and gets into all sorts of mischief and mayhem as a result. Or maybe your teen would like to grapple with the idea of what happens when science goes too far while reading *Frankenstein* (1818) by Mary Shelley or *The House of the Scorpion* (2002) by Nancy Farmer.

Don't forget to add in some meaningful experiments! There are many fabulous kits out there but I especially like the Thames and Kosmos series of science kits. Science experiments are an absolute requirement for studying science. Children need to experience science, not just read about it. With these elements in place, you have a solid science program built around living literature.

## Mathematics

I know you are thinking that math is the one subject that it would be difficult if not impossible to study with literature. But that is just not so! There are so many beautiful and entertaining living math books on the market! Math is often seen as a boring subject, but living books can add life to your math studies. Even the math haters can enjoy a well written picture book or puzzle game. Too often, math is seen as a boring and difficult subject that can only be taught with dry textbooks. But math is a natural entity that we use all of the time. So why not make it more interesting with living books? This is called Living Math – which is appropriate, since math is everywhere – it's a living, breathing subject!

A caveat: Living Math does not mean replacing a solid math course like Math Mammoth or Teaching Textbooks completely with living books. It means supplementing that program with living books to enhance the study of mathematics.

One of the things I instituted many years ago in our homeschool is Fun Math Fridays. Every Friday we skip our usual academic math lessons and we play a game or read a living book – I usually let the children choose. There are many quality math stories that can help you teach specific concepts. Two of my favorite series of math books are the *Mathstart* series and the *Sir Cumference* series. Both are a series of colorful picture books that each cover a specific math topic, from fractions to addition to percentages.

Greg Tang and Mitsumasa Anno have written many fantastic living math books as well. For upper elementary through middle grade ages, you might like to try Marilyn Burn's books like *Math for Smarty Pants* (1982) and *The I Hate Mathematics! Book* (1975). If you are looking for more of a math story, you can't go wrong with *The Number Devil: A Mathematical Adventure* (1997) by Hans Magnus Enzensberger or *The Adventures of Penrose the Mathematical Cat* (1997) by Theoni Pappas.

Some ideas for a Fun Math Friday to get you started:

- Math manipulatives – pattern blocks, tangrams, counting bears, dominoes or dice just get them out and let your child explore!

- Games – monopoly, Smath, card games like War, Uno or Rummy, dice games like Yahtzee

- Cooking – double, triple or even half a batch of cookies and let your child figure out the recipe's new measurements

- Look for patterns in nature on a nature walk

- Read a living book and then explore the topic more thoroughly with manipulatives

- Play with numbers outdoors with sidewalk chalk

- Explore with different kinds of calculators

- Play with a hundreds chart and let your child discover all the different patterns

- Have fun with rulers, yard sticks and measuring tape – measure everything!

- Keep a math journal – just like a nature journal – and have your child record their latest math discoveries.

There are so many ways to play with math – it never has to be a dull subject!

## Literature, Tales and Poetry

I'm a big believer in providing children with a banquet – rather than just reading nothing but history and historical fiction, I like to include plenty of great literature – classic works like *The Complete Tales of Winnie-the-Pooh* (1926), *Alice's Adventures in Wonderland* (1865), and *Charlotte's Web* (1952), as well as more modern reads like the *Harry Potter* series (1998-2009) by J.K. Rowling and *The Tale of Despereaux* (2003) by Kate DiCamillo.

Providing a variety of genres helps to expose children to all the different ways of telling a story. Maybe they'll discover a genre they never even knew existed! A couple of years ago, I read aloud *The Hitchhiker's Guide to the Galaxy* (1979) with my teens. One of my twin sons was riveted. This wasn't his first foray into science fiction – we had previously read *A Wrinkle in Time* (1962), but this was the first science fiction novel that truly captivated him. He went on to search out more books like that and even read *The Martian* (2011) completely on his own. He now says that science fiction is his favorite genre to read.

And don't forget poetry, tales and mythology! Poetry can feel daunting, but it doesn't need to. Many of us may feel like poetry is too difficult or only for the intellectually elite. But poetry is for everyone! Choose a quality book (I love the *Poetry for Young People* series, but there are so many lovely poetry anthologies on the market today) and just read a few poems over breakfast once or twice a week. When you're just starting out, don't worry about getting too involved, just read the poems and enjoy their sound and word play. Later, you can study one poet at a time, reading and getting an ear for their style.

Maybe give them the opportunity to play around with poetry of their own. I like the magnetic poetry you can just stick on the refrigerator – take turns throughout the day arranging the words to create a thrilling or silly poem. Learn about the rules for Haiku and Sonnets and then write your own. There will be time later for delving into analysis. Don't let that be a barrier to exploring poetry with your children. Just have fun with it.

Also don't discount fairy tales and mythology – they make up a huge amount of cultural literacy! I love the quote attributed to Albert Einstein that says:

*"If you want your children to be intelligent, read them fairy tales. If you want them to be more intelligent, read them more fairy tales."*

I would argue that the same goes for mythology. By exposing your child to these ancient tales, you are guiding them into a common language. Suddenly all those Disney movies make sense – they are nearly all based on fairy tales and mythology!

Shakespeare is also full of mythology; so many of his plays come straight out of Greek and Roman myth. Adaptations of so much of Shakespeare can be found in today's literature, movies and music. The more you expose your children to fairy tales, mythology and Shakespeare, the more culturally literate they will be, and the more they will get out of reading classic literature. We want them to be able to take part in The Great Conversation, in which they read and contemplate with the great thinkers and writers of Western Civilization. When those great thinkers first began writing down their ideas, those that came after read their works and grappled with those ideas in their own writing. Writers influenced other writers, and when your child reads those works, they too can join this "conversation."

But more than that, fairy tales and mythology teach your child about story structure, lessons in morality, critical thinking skills and so much more.

Yes, I brought up Shakespeare. So often, his works are looked at with fear or confusion. Yes, they are difficult, but not impossible to read. It's a matter of adjusting your ear to the language. After all, Shakespeare's plays were meant to be seen and heard, not read. But how do you approach Shakespeare with your children? Don't be intimidated! Even a novice can learn to love the bard.

First, choose a play to study. I like to start with either *A Midsummer Night's Dream* or *Macbeth* as both of these plays have great appeal for a young audience. Then read a children's version or retelling of the play. I like *Beautiful Stories from Shakespeare* (1907) by Edith Nesbit and *Shakespeare Stories* (1985) by Leon Garfield for this, but there are many children's versions of Shakespeare available on the market today. I like to start with a retelling because it gives you a good overview of the plot first without all the flowery language. This will make it so much easier for younger listeners to understand the point of the story.

Now that your child knows and understands the plot, start reading the actual play. We will often read it together, each taking a role (or two or three) in the play. Because there are often a lot of characters to keep track of, we will sometimes make a chart of how characters connect to each other. Sometimes we make little popsicle-stick style hand puppets to act out the play. We'll also each take a part to memorize – Shakespeare's plays are loaded with beautiful monologues to recite! Again, this is a great way to get theatrical. Acting out the plays around the kitchen table is a lot of fun.

If you are adventurous or have theater experience, you could put together a Shakespeare homeschool group and have the children act out a play. This ticks off so many items – theater, public speaking, language arts and literary analysis (discuss the play as you study the lines!) and of course, the dreaded "s" word of the homeschool world – **socialization**!

Finally, after you are all familiar with the story, you need to see the play. There are many fantastic movies that have been made based on Shakespeare's plays, but many have elements that might be inappropriate for your child. You will definitely want to preview them first. If you are lucky, you might even be able to see a live play. Remember, Shakespeare's plays were meant to be seen, so don't let your child only know the bard through reading his plays. Watching his plays performed brings a whole new element to the experience.

Educating with literature can be as structured or unstructured as you wish. It can be interest led or completely planned out for the entire school year. It can work with a 4 year old just as beautifully as it can work for a high school senior. You'll not only study a wide variety of material from writers who care about their subject matter, you'll also expose your children to The Great Conversation, to ideas beyond their own small world, to fantasy worlds filled with magic to the fascinating world that can only be seen under a microscope. It is all out there, just waiting to be discovered in a good book.

# Chapter 6 - Literary Language Arts

When it comes to language arts, living books are the most natural way to learn. When you learn through beautifully written literature, you don't need to use extra workbooks or textbooks to study language arts. Language arts encompasses many smaller subjects, and it can be overwhelming to study without a full curriculum. However, if you focus on the end goal, which is to have your child become an efficient communicator, it helps you to streamline all of those smaller parts into a coherent whole, and makes it so much easier to teach.

Why do we need to study language arts? What is the purpose?

The purpose is to learn to be able to communicate well. As we hope that our children will come to love reading, we also hope that they will learn to express their knowledge well. Being able to clearly and easily express ideas is an incredibly important skill. No matter what career they choose in the future, you can guarantee that good communication skills will be of the utmost importance. With that in mind, let's look at how we can study language arts through literature.

There are several components to language arts: reading (from phonics to literary analysis), writing (from forming letters to writing essays and stories), spelling, grammar, and vocabulary. It seems like so many plates to spin, but using literature and Charlotte Mason's philosophy as your base simplifies the subject. Narration, or telling back, is the basis for composition and literary analysis. Copywork and dictation can be used to teach everything from punctuation and mechanics, as well as parts of speech and spelling. You can study vocabulary in context as you are reading beautiful literature aloud to your children. And of course reading is taught with real books!

*Composition is as natural as jumping and running to children who have been allowed due use of books.* ~ *Charlotte Mason*

Living literature is truthfully all you need to give your children a thorough grounding in language arts skills. Now let's break down each of those sub-topics and see how we can study them with living books.

## Reading

Teaching your child to read is one of the first hurdles many of us stare at with anxiety at the beginning of our homeschooling adventures. This is often the litmus test we give ourselves, proving to the world whether or not we are capable of homeschooling our children. When perfect strangers and relatives alike discover you have made the decision to homeschool, they will inevitably ask you politely but with worried eyes, "But has he learned to read yet?"

However, reading is a developmental skill, much like speaking or walking or learning to use the toilet. Some children will read fluently and with very little instruction at the age of 4, others may not read at all until closer to 9 years old. It can be difficult to get out of the public-school mindset and allow your child to learn on their own timetable, especially with reading as it is such a fundamental skill, but it is essential to let it happen naturally. Just like you couldn't force your 12-month-old to walk, you cannot force your six-year-old to read.

Without a firm foundation of reading, our children cannot move ahead. So we may be tempted to spend hundreds of dollars on fancy phonics curricula, and waste many hours of time attempting to teach reading as if it were a science... But you taught your child to speak fluently without fancy educational materials, and you can do the same with reading.

Learning to read begins with learning what language looks like. This is why it is so important to read with your children as much as possible in the early years. Point to the words as you read them. Play with magnetic letters or alphabet blocks. Make sure you read quality literature and talk about the story as you read. Developing a "sense of story" is just as important as learning their letters. This is building the important skill of reading comprehension.

When a child is ready, either because they are asking to be taught to read or they are attempting to sound out words on their own, or even just showing a lot of interest in letters themselves, then you can begin formal reading instruction. I have taught all four of my children to read using BOB Books and *Teach Your Child to Read in 100 Easy Lessons* (1983). I found these materials to be invaluable and extremely simple to use, not to mention very economical. Generally, by lesson 60, my children were all reading well enough to move on to books like the *Little Bear* (1957) or the *Frog and Toad* (1970) series. Even though it isn't strictly Charlotte Mason inspired, I do like to supplement these further with the Explode the Code workbook series, which is a fantastic and easy to use phonics workbook series. The key to teaching reading is to expose your child to excellent quality picture books, and giving them the space to learn to read when they are ready.

You can also break up the reading lessons with fun and interesting games. My children all loved writing on our white board, so we would play hangman or just have fun playing with letters and sounding out silly words. Another fun idea that my children all enjoyed was playing with letter tiles. You can purchase these or make your own with a printer and laminator. Then let them play with the letters and form words to sound out. You could use the same idea and make word tiles and create silly sentences to read to each other. Play with words! Make it fun and interesting and it won't feel like schoolwork at all.

One of my sons was a late reader, and no amount of pushing made him pick up the skill of reading any faster. But when he turned 9, things seemed to just fall into place and now he is reading at the same level as his twin brother who learned to read at the age of 6. Being a late reader doesn't mean they are behind. It just means they weren't developmentally ready. Just remember, when they finally do begin to pick up the skill, let it happen naturally. Too much drill and practice can kill their natural desire to learn to read. I learned that the hard way.

You see, I mistakenly thought that my twins needed to stay on the same grade level. So when one was able to read fluently at 6 and the other wasn't, I panicked. I pushed my son and drilled, and we spent hours working on reading. Yet no amount of practice seemed to help. I regret all of that now. Looking back, I can see that pushing a child who isn't ready does far more harm than good. Yes, he can read now, and he is on grade level, but he doesn't really enjoy reading. I attribute that to the way I made reading a frustrating experience for him. If I could do it over again, I would have laid off the phonics drill and kill and just let him be.

Reading should never become a chore. Give them the tools and help that they need, but then back off and let them just enjoy their new skill.

Allowing them the freedom to choose their own reading material can mean all the difference in developing a love of reading. Trips to the library to choose new books to borrow should be seen as an exciting excursion. Sometimes they will choose well written, thought provoking books, but other times they'll choose what amounts to twaddle.

My rule has always been to allow them to choose whatever books they want. I don't forbid twaddle – we all enjoy a mindless read now and again, right? I just refuse to read it aloud. Give them the power over their reading and watch them grow into children who love to read.

## Narration

Narration is the backbone of language arts within the Charlotte Mason philosophy. At its core, narration is simply telling back what you read or heard. It is a way to sharpen listening and comprehension skills. Narration takes the place of reading comprehension and tests – you no longer need a list of questions to see if your child was listening or focusing on what they read.

So, for example, I might read an Aesop Fable to my child and then ask them to tell it back to me in their own words. Charlotte Mason didn't begin narrations until a child was 6 years old, so for a very young child, this sort of simple retelling is enough. Simply read a short story, or a brief excerpt from a longer story, and then ask the child to tell back what they heard. A few short sentences is enough for you to gauge if they were listening and if they were able to comprehend the basic idea of the story.

For a child who is new to the idea of narration, the first few times they might need some guidance – maybe ask them about a specific part of the story or write a list of key words from the reading on a white board to help them stay focused. It is important to remind them to use their own words – narration should not be the same as memorizing the story. Narration is about "ownership of knowledge". They need to learn to take something and make it their own.

If a child has a hard time focusing enough to narrate a full chapter or passage from a book, you can pause every other page or so to ask them about what is happening in the story. This way they aren't having to try to recall the whole thing at once, and it is training them to be able to focus on the reading. You can even offer them hints, such as, "What difficult decision did the main character just make?" or "Where is the main character heading now?" You can slowly stretch the length of the reading until they are comfortably listening and narrating a full chapter at a time.

Another thing to consider, is if the text is meaty or thought provoking enough to warrant a narration. If your child is struggling to find something to say about the reading, it might be possible that the reading didn't give them anything to say. Not all books need narrating. The idea isn't *just* to recall what they heard, but to take interesting information and make it their own.

As they get older and become better narrators, your child's narrations will develop and become more complex. At first their narrations will be very straightforward and "just the facts." But as they age and hone their skills, you'll see them make more complex connections and form opinions. Their narrations will likely start conversations and discussions about what they are reading. This is what makes a literary education so great.

When you read a book, or watch a movie, your instinct is to talk to someone about it. You might even write a review or take part in a book club. This too is a form of narrating. Children *need* to talk about things, so narrating comes naturally to them. Between the ages of 6 – 10, narrations can and should be mostly oral. Once they get to be about 10, or when their writing skills are becoming stronger, they should start writing their narrations down. For some children, this might happen as young as 8, but only if they are comfortably writing. If you have a reluctant writer, there is no need to rush them into composition.

Narration is the beginning of composition. In the beginning, it will be very brief. Where your older child can talk for 15 minutes straight about a book they just read, when asked to actually write their synopsis down, they may be reduced to only 3 sentences. But as they become more comfortable with writing down their thoughts, they will expand their written narrations. Remind them that writing is just a different way of communicating their ideas. Something that I've found helpful when first beginning written narrations is to write down their oral narrations for them. Then let them read over what they said. This gives them the opportunity to see their own words in writing. They may want to edit or add more information, but this is a great way to help them see that writing is just putting their thoughts to paper, not that much different than talking.

Over time they will be able to easily progress to writing essays. It's important to continue oral narrations at this age, as it will give them opportunities to organize their thoughts without the stress of also having to write them down.

Not all children think and learn in the same way, and it's important to change things up a bit to keep them interesting. Not every book needs narrating, and if you always ask them to just tell back what they heard with every single reading, they will quickly become bored, and possibly frustrated, with narration. Like anything, too much of a good thing can be overkill. I like to stick to one oral narration a day up to about age 10. I rotate the subject they'll be narrating to keep things interesting. Mondays we might narrate history, Tuesdays can be science. On Wednesday we'll narrate from our read aloud, and Thursday I'll ask them to tell me about the book they are reading on their own. Fridays I'll let them choose. I know that this goes against Charlotte Mason's teachings, as she required narration for every lesson. But in my experience with my own children, this led to eye-rolling and dramatic sighs. So, I adjusted to suit their needs.

This keeps things fresh and interesting. Around age 10, when they begin written narrations, we might do one written narration a week in place of an oral narration. Over the next few months we slowly whittle down the oral narrations in favor of written until most their narrated lessons are written compositions. Keep in mind that these aren't going to be 5 paragraph essays. Most their narrations at this age are 4 – 6 sentence paragraphs.

But what does narration look like? I can't speak for all children, but for mine, narration has taken many forms over the years. Not all narrating is just retelling the story back – to keep my children interested, I've given them options to keep things new and refreshing. Sometimes it's as simple as sketching a scene from the reading or putting on a puppet show based on what we read.

Other times we have written character journals, we've written letters between two characters (sometimes from completely different books!), and created board games based on the books we've read. One of my children's particular favorites is to design a Jeopardy style game based on books we've read. They love to be able to quiz me to see what I remember. None of these were overly complicated to put into action, yet they gave my children different ways to look at and analyze what they read.

As you use narration in your child's education, you will find that their listening skills become sharper. You'll see they are able to concentrate and give more focus to their studies, and when done on a regular basis, it will improve their writing skills. It is such a simple idea but it will reap huge rewards.

## Copywork

Copywork can seem deceptively simple. Give your child a sentence or two and have them copy it. It can seem like pointless busy work, but the benefits are tremendous.

First, copywork takes the place of traditional penmanship practice. Once a child learns how to write their letters comfortably, they are ready to start simple copywork. Begin with very simple words and phrases, working up to simple sentences and have them copy it in the best handwriting. It is important that they give their best effort. If you find them struggling, give them less to copy. In the beginning, it's OK if they only do one word per sitting as long as that one word is in their best handwriting. You can gradually increase the length of the model as they become more and more comfortable. It is extremely important to take their age into consideration. A typical 6-year-old isn't going to be able to copy a paragraph worth of writing with their best effort.

Copying models of good writing teaches your child what good writing looks like. Many of the world's greatest writers learned how to write through copywork. Jack London would copy out his favorite books in order to teach himself good writing; Benjamin Franklin would copy or outline essays and then try to recreate them on his own to see if he could write them better. By copying good writing, your child learns what good writing looks and feels like, thereby improving their own writing.

Studies* have shown that writing by hand engages the brain and aids in recall. It might be tempting to think that writing by hand is outdated and archaic in today's world of technology, but there are many benefits to writing things by hand. The physical act of writing can help you to remember information better and for longer periods of time. In younger children, writing by hand develops fine motor skills and strengthens hand-eye coordination.

In the elementary grade levels, copywork can even take the place of formal language arts curriculum. You can use copywork to teach mechanics, such as proper punctuation and capitalization, as well as spelling, vocabulary, careful handwriting and parts of speech. You can teach them different writing techniques, such as how to write dialogue, different literary devices (metaphors, alliteration, etc.) – there are so many different ways that it can help nurture your child's writing abilities. Just choose one thing at a time to focus on.

For a beginning 6-year-old, you might focus on beginning with a capital letter and ending punctuation. Your 9 or 10-year-old is ready to learn about parts of speech or how to format dialogue and attribution. You can teach parts of speech by having them use a different color for each as they copy the passage. For example, they might write the nouns in green, verbs in blue, and adjectives in orange. Focus on just one thing at a time, spending as much or as little time as necessary until they understand. This is natural learning. When you are using text from their favorite stories, it will bring life and interest to their lessons.

If you want to teach good writing to your children, then you need to provide them with beautiful writing to copy. Choose passages from well-written books, poetry, songs, etc. You can even use copywork to aid in memory work – have them carefully copy down the poems or speeches that they are working towards memorizing. I find that when we use our memory work as copywork it helps them to learn it quicker because they are using more of their senses – mind, hands, and eyes.

So what does copywork look like in a typical homeschool environment? For a young child, I write their copywork very neatly on the top of a sheet of their writing paper. I read it over with them, pointing out anything of note and have them copy it out in their best writing. If your child is a dawdler, you may wish to set a timer. It should take no longer than 10 minutes to complete. I usually sit alongside a young child to guide them as they write. Remember, keep the lesson short – dragging a lesson on too long will cause your child to lose interest, dawdle, and get lazy with their work.

For an older child, I like to write out their copywork on a white board. I will often use different colored markers to show them things I want them to remember – punctuation, parts of speech, etc. By highlighting them with different colors, they will be more likely to notice and pay attention. I recommend doing copywork three days per week.

---

> *"Children should transcribe favourite passages. --A certain sense of possession and delight may be added to this exercise if children are allowed to choose for transcription their favorite verse in one poem or another... But a book of their own, made up of their own chosen verses, should give them pleasure."* ~ Charlotte Mason

---

Remember, copywork isn't only for children! We can keep our own "Commonplace Books" where we can jot down quotes from our own readings that strike our fancy. I find that when I am copying down a passage from a novel or a famous quote that I want to remember, I focus more on neat handwriting than if I were just jotting down a grocery list or a quick to-do list. This is also a great excuse to buy yourself a lovely bound journal and some fancy pens. Not only is this good for our own self-education, it's encouraging for our children to see that we are learning too.

## Dictation

Dictation is the bulk of our language arts in the middle school years. I feel that dictation covers so many aspects of language arts that it genuinely can be the basis of any language arts program. It covers both grammar and spelling, not to mention exposure to great writing and literary techniques. Think of it as copywork on steroids.

Starting around age 10, I choose a passage to be studied for the week. These passages tend to come from whatever book we're currently reading aloud. I write the passage on our whiteboard on Monday morning and we go over it each day. We pull any words they think will be difficult and we practice them each day for spelling. We discuss the punctuation, capitalization, and anything else I think is worthy of note. They use the passage for copywork on Monday and Wednesday, and then I read the passage phrase by phrase while they write it down on Friday.

If they get all the spelling words correct, I erase them from the board. If not, we leave them up for another week and I give them a spelling quiz the following week. I also add words to the spelling list if they consistently ask me to spell them. This is essentially all we do for spelling.

Just for an example, the following is a passage from *Blood on the River* (2007) by Elisa Carbone:

*"You might have been born the biggest fish in the sea, but the skill and perseverance of those lower born than you can take you down and destroy you."*

The words we might choose to study from this passage are – might, perseverance, and destroy. We'll talk about why the comma was used, and I'll let them listen to me read the sentence and ask if they can "hear" the comma. (I pause for about 1 beat for a comma, 2 for a period.) If we're studying grammar, I'll have them underline all the nouns or verbs, or whichever part of speech we're working on.

For an older child, or a child used to doing a weekly dictation, you can give up to two studied dictation assignments each week. However, you won't want to do more than that – like copywork, less is better. This isn't about giving them tons of practice, but rather being sure that they are always giving their absolute best effort. They are more likely to do so if they aren't being bombarded with busy work.

These passages usually come from literature but also occasionally from history or science. I put the passage on the whiteboard, and the first day we go over it and choose words to practice, we discuss any interesting punctuation or grammar and anything else they find tricky. Then the next day, they get some time to study over it before I dictate the passage. If a passage is especially difficult, we might only do the one passage for the week.

Here's an example of a harder dictation from *The Adventures of Tom Sawyer* (1876) by Mark Twain:

*"When Tom reached the little isolated frame schoolhouse, he strode in briskly, with the manner of one who had come with all honest speed. He hung his hat on a peg and flung himself into his seat with business-like alacrity."*

The words we might choose to study here are: isolated, briskly, honest, business and alacrity. We might discuss how schoolhouse is one word, why we hyphenate business-like, the meaning of the word alacrity, and anything else the student might find challenging from this passage.

And that is it. So very simple yet also so rich and varied. Because the lessons come from books that they are currently reading (and hopefully enjoying!), the words will have meaning. By working on one or two passages of studied dictation a week, your child will gain far more grammar and writing skills than by studying tedious passages and endless fill-in-the-blank assignments in a typical grammar textbook. This is "meaningful learning".

# Grammar

That isn't to say that you shouldn't ever teach formal grammar. Yes, teaching it in context is a fantastic way to learn, but unless you are an expert on the subject, you are likely to miss things that your child will need to know. I like to study grammar in-depth just a handful of times over the years. I recommend studying it around age 8 or 9, again around the age of 12, and then once more at the beginning of the high school years. I find that this is plenty – it isn't a subject that warrants yearly study outside of copywork and dictation. But by covering it more in-depth at each level (elementary, middle grades, and high school) you give your child the foundation needed to be a good communicator.

As far as recommendations for programs go, in the elementary years I like *Easy Grammar*. It's a solid, no-frills program. In the middle grades, my children have really enjoyed *The Giggly Guide to Grammar* by Cathy Campbell and Ann Dumaresq. At this age level, I've found that my children tend to think they already know everything about grammar and find it tedious. But a book like *The Giggly Guide Grammar* makes it silly and fun, and I get a great deal less eye-rolling when it's time to study. At the high school level, you can go back to *Easy Grammar* and use their *Easy Grammar Plus* program that is written for Jr. High – Adult level.

# Vocabulary in Context

A wide vocabulary is a necessity to success in life – it will improve your child's ability to understand other people's ideas, to be able to read extensively (and comprehend what they read), and articulate their thoughts clearly to others. But I'm convinced that you do not need to purchase any additional curriculum in order to build your child's vocabulary.

You can easily develop your child's vocabulary through, you guessed it, reading great literature. When they learn a new word in context, and they see it repeatedly over time, they'll retain it and add it to their own vocabulary. Learning new words in context just makes sense. The words will come alive within a story and burrow into their mind.

For example – if I just asked my child to randomly define this list of words:

- ominous      -  perilous
- venture      -  slither

They will grab a dictionary and do the assignment, but within a few days, they will probably have forgotten those words entirely. But, if they were to also read this passage:

*"From there it's a simple matter of entering the
Mountains of Ignorance, full of perilous pitfalls and
ominous overtones – a land to which many venture
but few return, and whose evil demons slither slowly
from peak to peak in search of prey."* – The Phantom
Tollbooth (1961) by Norton Juster

Suddenly, that same list of words come to life and
make sense in a whole new way.

Even before your child learns to read, you can begin
developing their vocabulary, by reading them the best
literature you can find. But don't just stop there –
build your own vocabulary by peppering your
everyday chatter with big, delicious words. Instead of
saying that you enjoyed your meal, you might say
that dinner is "scrumptious."

Or instead of asking your child to be nice, you could
ask them to be "courteous", and rather than call
something beautiful, you might say it's "ravishing" or
"stunning." I'm a big believer in not talking down to
children. Don't be afraid of using big words –
dialogue with them about anything and everything
and explain when you use a strange word that they
might not understand.

So how do we study vocabulary with literature? I like
to pick out a few words from our literature or poetry,
words that leap out at me or that I think my children

may not know. I might jot them down on our white board or just keep the list tucked in the book we're reading for my own personal use. In the early years we just go over those words orally, usually before the reading, so they can listen for the new words. Keep it simple – just read over the word and talk about the meaning, see if your children can guess what the word means using context clues, maybe talk about how it was used in the story, or why the author might have chosen that particular word.

With an older child, you might want to do a bit more. Some things that I've done over the years:

- Write a few of the vocabulary words on a small white board or sheet of paper and just let them look it over before the reading. Let them guess what the words might mean. Then after the reading, have them look at their guesses, and decide whether they were right or wrong. Talk about what the real meaning of the word is and have them write the correct definition.

- Give your child the vocabulary words to define (after the reading), and then ask them to write them in an original sentence. Be careful not to do this too often, though, as it can quickly become tedious. I wouldn't do this more than once a week.

- You could also play computer games with the vocabulary words at Spelling City or Quizlet, which are both free websites at the time of this writing.

The most important thing, however, is to read, read, read! Studies** show that an average child needs to hear a word 14 times in order to use it fluently. What better way to expose them to language and all of its nuances than by reading beautiful literature!

*http://www.wsj.com/articles/SB10001424052748704631504575531932754922518

** http://www.smekenseducation.com/developing-core-vocabulary-for-each-academic-area.html

# Chapter 7 – Education in the Early Years

When my youngest child, Regina, was four I was often asked by well-meaning strangers and family members when I was going to start homeschooling her. I would typically say that I already was – but it probably didn't appear to be true. I hadn't done much in the way of formal curriculum with her yet. But that isn't to say that she wasn't learning.

Children under the age of six do not require formal schooling. This is a hard pill to swallow for the excited new homeschooling mother. But it is true nonetheless. Before age six, learning should be organic. Just playing and living life is enough. You don't need a curriculum. You don't need a guide. Just play, live life, and enjoy your little one. They aren't little for long, and there are many years of formal academics ahead of you both.

I remember when my oldest daughter was three and I had just read about this new and crazy idea called homeschooling. I was just dying to get started, and she was happy to play along with me. She was so excited about reading that she begged to be taught, so just shy of her fourth birthday I was teaching her to read.

When my twins were that age, they were a little bit less interested in doing anything that resembled school work. I waited until they were four, and while one of them took to school work like a duck to water, the other was hesitant. All he ever wanted to do was draw. I struggled with it, because in my mind, because they were twins, they needed to be doing the same thing. It was another year or so of stressing myself out before I finally cut both of us some slack and tried something different with him. Everyone was much happier.

Then came little Regina. She was (and still is!) a ball of energy. We nicknamed her shark because she could never stay still. She didn't even enjoy being read to because she had difficulty sitting still long enough to enjoy a whole story. She loved to draw and dance and sing. She would say hilarious things and loved being the center of attention. But at four, I didn't think she was ready for formal schooling yet. I learned from my older three children that it just wasn't necessary, and it certainly wasn't worth damaging her spirit. Forcing her to sit still and work would have been frustrating for both of us.

But that isn't to say I didn't teach her at all. At four, she knew her letters, could count to 10, knew many colors and shapes, and could draw some pretty amazing pictures. But she learned all those things through play and just talking with me.

When your baby is learning to crawl, then walk, they are learning naturally. You don't need a curriculum for that. When they learn how to talk, they learn it organically from listening to you and the other people in their life. So why do we think we need to use a formal program to learn how to count and say the alphabet?

## What should I do for the preschool years?

First and foremost, play! Learning happens all the time. Your preschooler should spend the bulk of their day in play. Limit screen time and just get out into the world and explore!

**Art!** We play with play-doh, markers, colored pencils, different colored construction paper, crayons, pastels, sidewalk chalk, watercolor paints, and finger paints. There is lots of exploring to be done in this department. Try out new things and don't be afraid of mess. I like to keep extra newspaper on hand for those messy projects. You could also use drop cloths used for painting. Just protect your environment, get your child a large apron to protect their clothing, and let them do their thing!

Letting your child explore with art is such an important activity. They will gain motor skills, build their imagination and stretch their creative muscles. Don't inhibit them by telling them the "right way" to do a project. Just give them the tools and let them explore. Let them enjoy the sensory experiences of gliding a crayon across paper, mixing blobs of paint colors together with their fingers, seeing water colors bleed together. These kinds of experiences can expand their knowledge of the bigger world and how things work.

**Read aloud** great picture books. Reading with your preschooler is so important. Reading with them teaches them vocabulary, story structure, and cause and effect. It builds their imagination and teaches them morals. Make frequent trips to your local library and explore all the different genres of books they have to offer. Don't limit it to just stories. Explore the non-fiction selections, poetry, fairy tales...there are so many fantastic books geared toward early learners.

**Count EVERYTHING.** How many grapes, cars, birds on the tree, Play-doh snakes, etc. You get the idea. Sometimes I like to throw in a little gentle math – if I take this one away, now how many are left? What if I give you two more? Now how many? You are building their math skills in a natural way and making it that much easier to introduce formal math curriculum later.

My youngest loved to **help in the kitchen** at that age, so whenever I was baking she was right there, ready to help. Her favorite was "pup cakes." Cooking goes along with those early math skills. They learn the importance of following directions, and you can expand on those early math skills by teaching them simple fractions by letting them measure the ingredients.

**Get outside** as much as possible. Exploring nature is a meaningful part of their education. Let them crawl around on the grass and explore the world around them. Collect pretty leaves, count acorns, look at birds and learn their names, play with bugs and catch frogs and let them splash in puddles. Take walks, not just in your neighborhood but in local parks and nature trails. Be sure to wear bug spray and dress appropriately for the weather, but then let them be. Fretting about getting dirty or getting hurt will hinder their learning here. They will get dirty and they'll probably scrape a knee or fall. It's ok. They will be find. Small children are resilient creatures. Don't let your worries make them fearful of exploring, but do be there to help them climb or explore a local pond.

Most importantly, **talk.** Try to answer their questions, and show your child that you can find answers in books or on the computer; watch movies and talk about what you liked or didn't like about them. Chat while you are out and about and talk about what you are doing and why. Don't talk down to your children – you can use big words, explain why you prefer to buy the organic apples over regular, or why you like a piece of art while you are visiting an art museum.

I'm not convinced that any formal schooling is necessary before the age of six. With plenty of time spent in play, reading lovely books with mom and dad, and exploring the world around them they are gaining a far greater education than they would filling in workbooks and drilling math facts. There is more than enough time for formal academics later.

Now, that sweet, bundle of energy four-year-old is now a spunky sassy eight-year-old. She still has trouble sitting still, but she's a wiz at math, still loves to draw and is just on the cusp of being a fluent reader. She's inquisitive and happy, and I have zero regrets about our relaxed unschooled early years.

# Chapter 8 - The Habit of Reading

*The most common and the monstrous defect
in the education of the day is that children
fail to acquire the habit of reading.* ~
Charlotte Mason

The most important thing we can do for our children is to instill in them the habit of reading. Reading is the foundation on which their entire education is built. From a young age, we need to not only teach them *how* to read, but how to LOVE to read. There is a world of words out there, just waiting to be discovered. We just need to show our children how to find it.

But how does one build a habit of reading for their child? It begins at infancy. From birth, we can read to our children. Treat books with respect, make space in your home for them to live. Fill your home with quality books, and take time each day to read them with your child. Keep a basket of board books within your toddler's reach and let them look at the pictures.

Don't stress too much if they chew them or play roughly, but do teach them to respect books and use them gently. Read them to your child frequently – you might tire quickly from reading *Goodnight Moon* 10 or 20 times in a row, but toddlers and preschoolers love repetition and will often request the same book over and over again.

If you're new to reading aloud, start with 20 minutes a day. Read 2 or 3 picture books at bedtime, or a chapter or two from a chapter book. Later, add in another read aloud time during the day, maybe after lunch.

When your child has learned to read to themselves, it's easy to want to drop that read aloud time. Don't! Reading aloud is such an important part of their education. It shouldn't stop just because they are capable of reading by themselves. Continue your regular read aloud times, but add in another "quiet reading" time for them to read on their own. During this quiet reading time, both you and your child should be reading something. In order to build the habit of reading in our children, we have to first build the habit of reading in ourselves. It doesn't matter if you are reading Charles Dickens or James Patterson, just read *something*.

Let them see that you think reading is important and worthy of your time. If you treat reading as a chore – just another thing to check off your to-do list – your child will come to regard reading as work. It's a sad fact that many people grow up despising reading, and never read another book once they're finished with school.

What do you do if your child already thinks reading is boring? Sometimes, despite our good intentions, our children just don't enjoy reading. Maybe they've been in school and had dull books forced on them, or their teachers pushed literary analysis too early. Maybe you did everything right and they still just don't enjoy it. What then?

Choose the most interesting, fun, exciting books you can find. I spent a year reading aloud all of the Harry Potter books with my twins. I could have made them read them on their own – they are capable. But, they would have rather just watched the movies and been done with it. Reading the books seemed like work to them, and why bother with the extra work of reading when the movies were so much more efficient?  I convinced them that the books were a much better experience, because they contained the full story, so we read them together. It was the first time in years that they begged me to keep reading, and I relished it. Sometimes you just need to find the right books.

Talk to your child and find out what their passions are. What do they get excited about? Find books to match their interests. If all they are interested in is video games, get them a subscription to a gamer magazine. Find them game manuals to read. Introduce them to comics, mythology, and fantasy – all important elements to gaming. If they are teens, give them the book *Ready Player One* (2011) by Ernest

Cline. This novel about a future where everyone spends most their time in virtual reality gaming world got my twins very excited about reading.

Make regular trips to your local library. Don't force them to check out anything specific. Just let them browse. I like to play a game with my daughter when she gets stuck figuring out what to choose. We go in the middle of an aisle, she closes her eyes and spins around 3 times, then puts out her hand. Whatever book she touches, she has to check out. Sometimes it's a dud, sometimes it's a book she's already read, but occasionally, she finds something wonderful. If your child requests guidance, maybe give them specific parameters, like a book of poetry, or a book about a famous person you've never heard of before. This gives them a place to start if they are overwhelmed by the huge selection of books.

If they've been thinking about a topic or immersed in a particular subject lately, guide them to the section of the library where they might find more information. One of my children spent one summer reading every single book about dinosaurs he could find in our library. Again, don't force them to choose anything, but give them the opportunity to see what is available.

Let them take out whatever strikes their fancy, even if it's something you yourself wouldn't think of as "quality" reading. Giving them ownership of their reading choices will allow them to have power over their education. Yes, they might bring home many cartoon character type books, but eventually, when they have learned to have an ear and eye for what great literature sounds and looks like, they will check those types of books out less and less.

When my daughter was around 11, she fell in love with a popular book series. I read the first few books so I could see what she was reading and I was shocked by how terrible the writing was. The plot was interesting enough in the first couple of books, but it was bogged down in bad writing and awful characterization. I asked her why she liked it, and she thought the story was fun, and she liked the fantastical aspects of the story. She asked my opinion, and I shared what I liked and disliked about the books. She was surprised that I thought the writing was bad, but wasn't deterred from continuing the series.

Flash-forward to this past summer. She was excited to see at our library that the author had written another book in the series that she didn't know about, so she eagerly brought it home and dove into the story, expecting to feel waves of nostalgia. Later that day she dropped the book back into the library basket, disappointed. She was surprised at how bad the writing was, and mused that she didn't recall it being that awful when she was a kid. I was secretly pleased that she came to that conclusion. Years of surrounding her with well-written living literature had given her the ability to spot bad writing, even where she couldn't see it in the past.

Make reading times special. Once you've chosen books to read, make reading them a special experience. Bake cookies, make some hot chocolate, snuggle up together and enjoy the story. Create an atmosphere in which reading becomes a memorable part of your day. Something you all look forward to when you wake up in the morning. It may not happen right away, but when you live in a literature immersed world, and you make reading a pleasurable experience, your child will come to regard reading as something to be enjoyed rather than something they HAVE to do.

The one thing you absolutely should not do, especially if your child already dislikes reading, is make reading into school work. Do not give them writing assignments, ask too many questions, or require anything but their attention. There is time for all of that later. If they want to write about a book, that's fantastic.

But making your reluctant reader write about a book is a sure fire way to kill the love of reading. Never make it into work. Just read and enjoy. Talk about what you like about the story, talk about the choices the characters are making, talk about what you think might happen next, but that is all that is necessary. Keep it fun and casual. Anything more is overkill.

It can be especially tempting with older children to make reading into a school assignment. What I do with my reluctant readers is to only assign writing to subjects they enjoy. So we'll write about science and history, and sometimes I ask them to write about a documentary that we've watched. This keeps reading as a sacred activity. When they know that they won't be forced to analyze every book they read, it makes reading so much more relaxing. And that is exactly what reading should be! You can still sneak in some narration of course – but do it in a way that they don't realize that they are narrating.

When we read together, discussion naturally flows – we talk about the decisions the character made, how they would react in the same situation, why a certain setting makes sense for the story, what they think might happen next. This is narrating without calling it narration! If it is a book they are reading on their own – you should try to read it too. Then you can talk to them about the story. Often, when given a well-written book, your child will come to you to tell you all about it.

Another way to add an element of fun to reading is to make it a social experience. The best way to do that is to start or join a book club. If you are lucky enough to have a great library nearby, you can often find an age appropriate book club to join. But it's easy to start one yourself. Just put out the word within your homeschool community that you want to start a book discussion group and then choose a book to read and discuss.

Sometimes just the fact that their friends are reading the same book as they are inspires them to think more about the books they are reading. Book clubs are a great way to get deeper perspective on literature, and they are fun too! Why not make it even more interesting by adding in cosplay (dressing up as a favorite character from the story), book related treats (for example: whip up some butterbeer and pumpkin pasties when reading Harry Potter), or play book trivia games.

If you can instill the habit of reading in your child, they can, and will, succeed in life. They'll be able to learn anything their heart desires, because they'll know how to find the information. Reading will open doors and worlds and inspire them to join into the Great Conversation and lead to a lifetime of learning.

*"So much for the right books; the right use of them is another matter. The children must enjoy the book. The ideas it holds must each make that sudden, delightful impact upon their minds, must cause that intellectual stir, which mark the inception of an idea."*
~ *Charlotte Mason*

# Chapter 9 - A Happy Mess: An Outlet for Creativity

This chapter may feel a bit out of place in a book about giving your child a literary education, but bear with me. Young children are extremely creative. It isn't until they go off to school that the creativity is leeched out of them by the tedium and monotony of lessons. However, the world needs creative individuals for society to grow and thrive and improve. Without creative individuals like Steve Jobs and Jim Henson, the world would be a much different place. It's easy to think that creativity is only for those special, gifted artists and musicians, but all of us can learn to add creativity into our day. Anyone can be creative, given the right outlet.

So how do we encourage that creativity? Small children are full of imaginative ideas. Give them some blank paper and crayons and they'll draw the most fantastic pictures. Throw in a large empty box and some scarves and they can happily play for hours on end. It is simple when they are small as there is very little hindering their creativity at that age. They haven't yet learned to watch hours of television or become addicted to video games and technology. Before the age of 4, there isn't that much you need to do to encourage creativity – it blossoms within them. But if I were to give you one tidbit of advice for this age range, it would be to severely limit screen time. Small children just do not need to watch television for hours at a time, nor do they need to have constant access to a smart phone or tablet. Just let them play with open-ended toys and read plenty of picture books.

It's not until they reach school age that children will begin to lose a bit of their imagination. Hours spent in a classroom being told the correct way to create or all of their free time spent zoning out in front of a television or playing video games will siphon the imagination right out of them. But because we are homeschoolers, we have more control over their day-to-day activities and therefore we have the power to inspire them to learn to "think outside of the box." Given the right tools, our children can learn to hone their creative powers and develop them in new and exciting ways.

Start by giving your child access to plenty of art supplies. With four kids, we buy printer paper by the case and let them have at it. You don't need to save every doodle or scribble, just a few favorites, but let them draw until their hearts are content. I like to set up a corner in my kitchen where my children can easily get to whatever materials they need – crayons, pencils, markers, paints, a variety of paper, stickers, and modeling clay. When inspiration strikes, they can get right to the business of creating without having to wait for an adult to get them what they need.

If you are worried that they'll make a mess – well they will. But a few lessons on proper use of markers and paints will go a long way to saving your sanity and building their creative muscles. Teach them where to put everything back when they are done. But don't let your fear of mess prevent them from being able to explore colors and techniques. Creativity is messy. So give them a prepared area where they are free to make a mess.

They will go through reams of paper. I used to joke with my husband that my children must have required an entire forest for their art work. It seemed like they would go through reams of paper every day. I like to buy cases of paper in the late summer when the back-to-school sales are going and we can stock up for the year for a reasonable price. I will make sure we have some nice thick paper for painting, as well as a stash of old newspapers to put out to catch paint drips.

There is more to art than just painting and drawing –
provide them with blocks, Legos, Duplos (Legos
larger and far less deadly when-stepped-upon cousin)
and other building sets. One of the best toy
investments we made when my children were small
was a set of Wedgits. We started with the small set,
and expanded from there. We now have a huge tub of
Wedgits, and everyone from my husband on down to
the eight year old loves to build with them. My boys
recently got into Legos, so we now have several sets
for them to tinker with. Blocks of all types give
children something to do with their hands while they
are listening to read alouds, or music, or just playing
in their free time. Building is a creative endeavor.
Playing with blocks of all types will develop their
motor skills and hand-eye coordination; promotes
spatial skills, math skills, creative problem solving,
and more. The benefits are massive, so let them build.

To inspire their creative expression, I introduce my
children to great art. I want them to have a familiarity
with great works of art. I try to tie our art
appreciation to our history cycle, so that everything
connects. I'm a big believer in strewing my children's
path with books and materials that fit together, giving

them deeper connections than if we just studied art and music randomly.

So, if we're studying the Renaissance, we'll look at art from Leonardo da Vinci, Michelangelo, and Botticelli. I like to focus on one artist for a three – four week period, longer if my children are interested, and get a look at a range of that artist's works. I highly recommend scouring library book sales and thrift stores for books about specific artists or periods of art.

I've gotten some gorgeous oversized coffee table type books with big glossy pictures of famous works of art for under a dollar at these sales. If you can't seem to find any good ones, the internet is a treasure trove of pictures of artwork. You might also look for calendars that focus on famous artists. Also check your library to see if they have art books to borrow, as well as biographies about the artists for you and your child to read together.

So how do you study the art? I like to choose a piece for them to study – I'll open the book to the piece we're studying and display it in a prominent place. We'll look at it together, talking about the painting – pointing out the colors, how the artist used light or dark, if it looks realistic or not, and so on. Sometimes we'll make up a story about the painting or try to decide what the person in the portrait is thinking. The painting is one snapshot in time. What happened in the scene before? What could happen in scenes later?

I'm a big fan of Maryann F. Kohl's books – *Discovering Great Artists* (1996) and *Great American Artists for Kids* (2008). We'll often choose a project from one of those books, though occasionally, we will try our hand at copying one of the pieces we studied during the week. Another fantastic art history resource is the book *Vincent's Starry Night and Other Stories: A Child's History of Art* (2016) by Michael Bird. Going chronologically through history from prehistoric man through the modern day, each short chapter focuses on one piece of art. My children enjoy the stories, and we all learn more about the artist, the time-period, and more. It's quickly becoming one of our family favorites. Once or twice a year, we like to take a trip to the local art museum, so they can see some of the artwork they've been studying throughout the year "in person."

And what about music? I approach music appreciation in much the same way as we study art. We'll choose a composer and listen to some of their works, read a bit about their life, either in a picture book or if there isn't one, I'll do some research and narrate back to them what I learned. While I'll occasionally play our current composer as background music during their lessons, they need to have a focused listening time as well. We'll talk about the music – how does it make them feel? What instruments do they hear? What do you think this song is about? Could you create a story or lyrics to go with it? If this song were a painting, what might it look like? This is both training their ear as well as flexing their creative muscles.

But music is more than just classical composers. We explore different genres, from jazz to rock to Broadway show tunes. We might focus on one particular genre for a few weeks, especially if my children are enjoying it. My husband and I like to expose our children to our personal favorites as well – Led Zeppelin, Pearl Jam, Cindi Lauper, David Bowie, and Nirvana. Great music is subjective. Whenever possible, we try to take our children to a live concert. Our children have been to dozens of shows, from huge arena concerts to small venues where they can sit right in front of the stage. Being able to hear live music is an awesome experience, especially for aspiring musicians.

And of course, our children should be encouraged to make music of their own. Our children chose instruments between the ages of 7 and 9, so we currently have a guitarist, two drummers and a pianist. My guitarist and oldest drummer are also taking piano lessons as well, as they have dreams of attending Berklee College of Music in Boston, and were told by an instructor that being proficient in piano would be helpful and make them more well-rounded musically. Recently my youngest decided she needed to take piano as well, so now three of my children are studying two instruments each.

I encourage our children to practice for a minimum of one hour every day. For those who aren't serious about music study, this is plenty. But for the serious musician, they might spend 4 – 5 hours focusing on their music each day. Like the art supplies, musical instruments should be easily accessible. Allowing freedom to practice will often lead to them practicing far more than if they were restricted to a specific time of day. Giving my children the freedom to practice as much as they like has led to my boys working together to create original music, and my daughter figuring out how to play songs by ear.

There are so many other activities that fall under the category of creativity – theater, cooking, writing, dance. There is a world of activities to explore. I like to give my children the freedom to dabble. They can take a few classes here and there, play around with video equipment, write a fan-fic blog, and create their own recipes. When you utilize short, focused lessons in the mornings, the afternoons can be free for these sorts of creative endeavors. These activities are more than just hobbies or electives – they are opportunities for your children to develop their talents and discover new passions. You never know, you may be raising the next coming of J.K. Rowling, Stan Lee, Jim Henson, or John Bonham!

# Chapter 10 - Getting into the Out-of-Doors

When you've explored the Charlotte Mason method for a little while, you quickly see that Nature Study is one of her philosophy's major concepts. She encouraged parents and teachers to get their students outside for hours at a time, not just to study nature, but to take walks, hikes, and just enjoy the outdoors. On paper, this makes sense – we were made to be outdoors, we absorb vitamin D from sunshine, fresh air is good for everyone, and children generally love playing outside. However, this was nearly the deal breaker for me. I had the hardest time in the beginning, figuring out how to implement Nature Study into our days.

> *Every common miracle which the child sees with his own eyes makes of him for the moment another Newton.* ~ *Charlotte Mason*

For starters, I am most decidedly an "indoor girl." While I love the idea of getting out into nature, I'm terrified of many insects and squeamish about playing in the mud. Not to mention that weather is often prohibitive – I live in the Northeast, so we tend to have long snowy winters where all anyone in my house wants to do is hibernate. While I am happy to send my children outside to burn off some of their excess energy, I was never quite sure how to use that time productively to study nature. My children were happily running amok, riding their bikes and playing tag. How do you turn that into a study of nature? I worried about making playing outside too "schooly."

But it turns out, it's not nearly as difficult as I had first thought. Children are naturally delighted with the world out-of-doors. They would discover things and bring them to me, and if I didn't know what it was, we could look it up in a field guide. In the beginning, I was carrying a bag full of field guides when we would take walks so that I could look things up on the fly. Nowadays I just use my smartphone. I kept it very relaxed and simple. We'd play in the yard or go for a walk, and I'd ask them to find something they thought was pretty. Then we'd find out what their discovery was called and draw a picture in a notebook. Easy peasy!

As we got used to doing this, I began to request more detail from my children. We started noting where they discovered their found item, what the weather was like that day, and any other detailed information they could discover. I didn't make it overly complicated, but I wanted them to be a little bit more observant about their surroundings.

But why is studying nature so important? In our modern society, where STEM rules, it seems almost silly to focus so much on nature. But nature study can be the foundation for all the other sciences to build upon. The child who has spent time exploring the natural world and learning the local flora and fauna will be ahead of the game when it comes to studying biology, chemistry and physics down the road. You can touch on so many things while observing the wonders of the natural world. From the mathematical principle of the golden ratio found throughout nature to the various life cycles of plants and animals, there is a never-ending wealth of information to be found quite literally in your own backyard.

Not only that, but studying nature will help to build both your child's attention span and observation skills. In a modern world where fast-paced media rules, it is so important for us to guide our children into the quiet world of nature. We all want to reduce the siren song of screens when it comes to how our children spend their time. Taking them out of doors for a walk or just a good dig in a mud puddle can do so much for them both mentally and emotionally.

Spending time outside can excite your child's natural curiosity about the world around them, leading them down rabbit trails to learning about things you never would have thought to include in your lesson plans.

> *"Let them once get in touch with Nature, and a habit is formed which will be a source of delight through life. We were all meant to be naturalists, each in his degree, and it is inexcusable to live in a world so full of the marvels of plant and animal life and to care for none of these things." – Charlotte Mason*

If you are anything like me, you are probably thinking that including nature study in your homeschool routine is going to be next to impossible. There is already so much on your plate! How will you ever make room for spending hours in the outdoors? My philosophy when it comes to studying nature is to do what works best for your family. If you live in an apartment complex in the city, you will need to make a much more significant effort to study nature than if you lived in a farmhouse in the country. You need to do what works best for you and your circumstances.

There honestly is no right or wrong way to study nature.

First, like anything else you want to include in your homeschool routine, you need to find a place for it. Aim for once a week to get you and your children outdoors. Even if only for one hour, get outside and explore. Because weather can be unpredictable, you can keep it as a floating weekly hour, though if you are prepared with the appropriate clothing, you can go out in any weather.

Second, you need to have a plan. Just going out and telling your child to look at nature will result in them wandering aimlessly. You can choose one particular feature of nature to study, such as fungi, birds, or trees. I like focusing on just one thing, because it gives your child something direct to look for and hone their observation skills. Take along a field guide, a notebook (or loose paper on a clip board), and a pencil and go exploring together.

Notice that I said "together." Nature study isn't an independent learning activity. You will need to participate with your child. If you lead by example, your child will learn to follow along in good habits. Much like showing them that reading is important by letting them see you read, show them that nature study is important by exploring, getting excited about what you find, and sketching your discoveries in your own nature journal.

My favorite book for getting started in nature study is *Nature Connection* by Clare Walker Leslie. This book is a fabulous resource if you aren't sure how to get out in nature. She gives you easy to implement activities and ideas, as well as activity pages that you can reproduce and add to your child's journal.

For a more in depth resource, you want to pick up *Coyote's Guide to Connecting with Nature* by Jon Young, Ellen Haas, and Even McGowan. This book is a guidebook for parents wanting to help their children connect with nature. Coyote's Guide gives you the tools to inspire curiosity and gives you the confidence to take risks and have adventures with your children in nature.

*The One Small Square* series by Donald Silver is a fantastic series of books as well. In each of the books in this series, the author explores a literal small square of various biomes – from the familiar (Woods, Pond, Backyard) to the far away (Arctic Tundra, Cactus Desert, Tropical Rainforest). Start with *Backyard,* and then choose a book that covers a nearby biome you would like to learn more about. Each book includes an abundance of information, beautifully drawn pictures, and activities that are easy to reproduce.

You'll also want to invest in a good set of colored pencils so that they can do their best artwork in their journals. I like Prismacolor pencils; the colors are vibrant and easy to blend and they are very excellent quality. Some other items to have on hand might be binoculars, a magnifying glass, and small plastic baggies to bring home specimens that you would like to study further. I like to keep the things we'll need for a nature walk in a small bag that we take along with us. This way everything is on hand and ready to go.

If you have a smart phone or tablet, I recommend downloading a few apps to help you identify things you find while studying nature. They are much handier than packing a bag full of field guides! I like the Audubon Birds of North America app – it uses your location to show you birds local to your area, and you can add your own sightings to help other bird enthusiasts to find local birds. I also like PlantNet Plant Identification for identifying plants in the wild. National Geographic has several apps you might like to check out as well. I love that we have so much fantastic technology at our fingertips that can aid our learning in the outdoors.

Also, don't forget to take field trips. While you can get quite a lot of nature study done in your own backyard or neighborhood park, it can be fantastic to change things up and go somewhere new. Especially if you are new to studying nature, going somewhere new can ignite a fire for both you and your child. Go on a trip to a local nature center or Botanical Garden. Maybe you have an Audubon center nearby or a Fish Hatchery. Take a trip (and bring along your drawing supplies!) and learn something new. Take a hike at a nature preserve, go to a state park, the beach. Even a trip to the local zoo can count towards nature study!

Don't be afraid to get dirty! Climb trees, lay on the ground and carefully look at the world beneath your feet, stalk birds and insects. Dress appropriately for the planned activity and wear plenty of sunscreen and bug spray. It is important that you not let your fear of dirt or scraped knees keep your child from getting down on the ground or up a tree and exploring the world outdoors.

Going out into nature might even inspire your child to begin a collection. Children love to collect things, so why not encourage them to collect rocks, leaves, or wildflowers? My children have collected leaves, rocks, seashells and fossils over the years. Give them the proper means to store their collection, maybe a shadow box or a scrapbook. This will show them that you take their collecting seriously.

For a quick and easy activity, create a visual scavenger hunt list before your outing and see how many items you can check off the list from red birds to white rocks to animals with 4 feet. Come up with 10-20 items based on your child's age, attention span and how long you plan on staying outside. Have fun with it!

If you, like me, have children who are obsessed with gaming, they might enjoy getting into geocaching. This is a type of scavenger hunt that requires you to download an app to your smartphone or tablet and use GPS to locate little treasures that people have hidden. We were excited to discover someone on our very own street had hidden one! You can find them anywhere and everywhere and even hide your own to get in on the fun. This is a fun way to get a reluctant child outdoors and exploring.

Don't forget to include a study of famous naturalists every once in a while. There are many quality picture books about naturalists that will inspire your children, from John James Audubon (*The Boy Who Drew Birds* (2004)by Jacqueline Davies), Wilson Bentley (*Snowflake Bentley* (1998) by Jacqueline Briggs Martin), and Jane Goodall (*The Watcher* (2011) by Jeanette Winter). Read one book every few months or so and introduce your child to someone who spent their life in a specific nature science field. Then, have your child work on a project inspired by that naturalist.

For example, my son was enthralled with the works of John James Audubon. One winter he set up camp in our front window, where he had an excellent view of our bird feeder, and drew every type of bird that visited. I helped him to identify each bird and he carefully labeled his drawings. He ended up with a big stack of drawings that we bound into a book.

Studying nature doesn't have to be intimidating. Take it slow, study together and you will find it to be an enjoyable experience for everyone.

# Chapter 11 - Putting It All Together: Creating Rhythm to your Days

What do you see when you picture your perfect homeschool day? When I first started out, I expected my children to work diligently at whatever assignment I gave them, listen intently to the books I chose to read aloud, and generally become brilliant and engaging children who were appreciative of all of the hard work and dedication I put into their educations. Then I was slapped with a reality stick and realized that I had to readjust my expectations.

Most of us have extremely high expectations about what homeschooling will look like, especially when we first start out. Maybe we have heard stories about homeschooled prodigies who went to college when they were 12, or we spend time on web forums or reading blogs about amazing homeschool families doing fascinating projects or winning spelling bees all while living in immaculately cleaned and organized homes.

All families are different, and blogs and forums can be deceiving – they are more apt to share the many successes without mentioning any of their failures. The most important thing to remember is that you have to be flexible. All children are different, they all learn on their own, individual time tables. The key to having a successful homeschool is to keep in mind that things will not always go as expected, so always leave wiggle room in your plans.

But that is not to say that you can't have wonderful homeschool days the majority of the time. Therefore, it is important to create a rhythm – I dislike the word schedule. I much prefer the idea of having a steady rhythm to our day. It brings to mind the image of a flowing river, gradually making its way to the sea. Rivers aren't in a hurry to get where they are going, and we shouldn't be rushing our children to be on any time table either.

Especially when you are new to a literature-based lifestyle of learning, it can be tricky to figure out how to plan out your day. And when you look at the list of what you want to accomplish daily: math, spelling, grammar, copywork, poetry, memory work, read aloud, history, art… well, you get the idea. It can easily become overwhelming. But it doesn't have to be!

Let's walk through a typical day in a literature-based homeschool. During the school year, it is wise to try to enforce an early bedtime so that you can begin your day at a reasonable time – try to aim for an early start time, like 8 or 9 o'clock in the morning. While homeschooling is more efficient than public school, it still takes several hours of your day. Getting an early start ensures that you will have plenty of free time in the afternoons for activities, leisure, or errands.

I'll give you a glimpse into a typical day in our homeschool, so you can get an idea of what a literature-based, Charlotte Mason inspired day might look like. I am currently homeschooling a 17-year-old, two 14-year-olds and an 8-year-old. My oldest does all of her school work online with an online liberal arts school and my twins take art and music classes at our local high school 3 days a week.

As I serve my children their breakfast, I make myself a cup of tea and grab our current reading – I usually do poetry, tales or mythology over breakfast. As they eat, I read and then we discuss. Sometimes it's a quick narration but other mornings we follow rabbit trails or have deeper discussions. Then I send everyone to get dressed and we dive into the rest of our daily activities.

My oldest teen is fairly independent. She joins us for read alouds, but otherwise, she's doing her own thing. I check in with her right after breakfast to discuss the day's assignments, and we'll talk off and on throughout the day if she needs anything or to discuss a lesson or a book she's reading, but otherwise, she just takes her work to her room or the kitchen table and gets it done. She didn't become independent overnight – I worked with her over several years to keep to a schedule.

I highly recommend that around the age 11 or 12, you start giving your child a check list of all their assignments. In the beginning, write them in order of priority – things that absolutely must be done go at the top, and then extra enrichment type activities go at the end. This gives your child an understanding of how to prioritize their time so that they can get their school work done efficiently. Gradually over the course of the next year or two, show them how to plan their own assignments. If you maintain a steady rhythm, it's easy to know what to do and when. This will make it that much easier for your teen to take on the responsibility of their own education. It will also ease their transition to college and beyond.

Back to our school day: Meanwhile if it is a "school" day, my twins are at school for their enrichment classes. If they are home, they are alternating math and music practice. With everyone else otherwise occupied, I sit down with my youngest, who is eight, and we read from her basket of books. We do a monthly theme for her morning basket – I try to alternate each month to keep things fresh. The themes we have covered this year, so far, are Thanksgiving, Space, Ancient Greece, Ancient China, and we are currently reading about anatomy and Ancient Rome.

I also include a literature read aloud, poetry, and art study, using *Vincent's Starry Night and Other Stories about Art* (2016) by Michael Bird. Sometimes she'll be inspired to draw a picture about what we've been reading, or we'll color a map or she'll create a small book about a topic she's excited about. I try to keep it pretty low-key at this age. Mostly we read and discuss.

Sometimes I'll plan a fun art project or a science experiment, and if the weather is nice, we'll take a walk or sit outside and find something to add to her nature journal. But for the most part, she just listens to stories and plays. In addition to this, she does daily reading lessons and math. Two or three days a week we also do copywork, and because she enjoys workbooks, we also do a few pages of *Explode the Code* to work on phonics rules. We spend maybe 15 minutes a day on seat work. I like to keep it very relaxed in the early years. There will be more than enough time for "real" academics later. Overall, her entire school day takes about an hour to an hour and a half.

By this time the twins are ready to move on to the next activity, so I've put the week's dictation on the board and we go through it together – the first day we look it over and make note of any words they need to practice spelling, any interesting punctuation, we might do a quick grammar study, and then they carefully copy it down. If there were words they needed to practice, they'll copy them down 5 times each. If it is a "school day" they do this in the afternoon when they are home.

I also like to have some sort of writing prompt on the whiteboard at least once a week – usually on Fridays – just something to stimulate creative writing. I like the book *Unjournaling: Daily Writing Exercises That Are Not Personal, Not Introspective, Not Boring!* (2006) Even my oldest likes to join in for this – they're usually genuinely interesting, thought provoking or silly – nothing overly personal (just try to get my boys to write about their feelings – it's not going to work!).

When they've finished this, I send them to do their silent reading and if it's a narration day (I assign these

3 days out of the week), they'll choose a narration card and do the assignment. These are almost always done in writing at their age, and it serves as their composition. Once or twice a month, I'll assign them a more formal writing assignment. These we revise, edit and polish up to be their absolute best work.

This is high school level writing, so we'll work through all the steps – gathering their information, narrowing their topic, writing an outline, writing the first draft, revising and editing and then finally, typing up their final draft. We start working on more formal writing around the age of 10, starting with a solid paragraph. By the time they are 12 or 13, I expect that they can write solid 2-page paper. I do use a curriculum to guide us in formal writing – my personal favorite is Susan Wise Bauer's *Writing with Skill series*. It can be dry at times but it gets the job done.

By now, it's around noon so its lunch time and we dive into our current read aloud. This is also when we go over memory work – we'll take turns around the table and everyone gets a chance to practice.

After lunch, we'll do the day's history or geography assignment, and/or science lesson. This is what I consider to be the fun part of our day. We'll discuss the reading, complete any activities or projects, look at our giant wall map and talk about where things were happening in our lessons, look up links from our reading, work on a research project, do an experiment, write a short report, or add to our timeline. We don't do all of these things every day – some days we only read a chapter from our spine book and discuss the reading. Some days we might complete map work, timeline work and a science experiment. If it's an art day, we'll complete an art project here as well. This is the meat of our days – it takes us anywhere from 45 minutes to 2 hours.

After this, we've finished our school day and the kids are free to scatter. Some days we're done by 1pm, others it's more like 3. But it doesn't feel like we've been grueling away for hours and hours. It's actually pretty relaxed. We still get a great deal accomplished! And there is quite a bit of flexibility here – this is an example of an average day, obviously, some days will look quite different.

The days my twins must be at school for a few hours can throw our routine out of whack; it has been an adjustment period this year. So there were many days that we just read and did math and called it good.

Some days we are out of the house for other activities so all that gets done is math and we might double up on reading the next day. Some days I might call a 'fun' day and we just do art projects, read, watch a movie, play board games or take a nature walk. It's all about rhythm and finding the flow that fits your family best.

The rest of our day is open to us – the children are free to work on their personal side projects. Currently the boys are spending the majority of their free time either practicing their instruments or working on writing and drawing their own graphic novels. My oldest is working on writing a blog, filming videos for her YouTube channel (Wonderful Meep – if you want to look her up) and writing a novel. My youngest draws pictures for hours on end and creates the most hilarious and bizarre "comic book" characters.

Meanwhile I can finish up housework, work on lesson plans, check in on the internet, sneak in some extra personal reading time and whatnot before I have to cook dinner. Over dinner, their father will ask them to tell something they learned that day. Everyone is expected to tell something different and add to the discussion. It's a fun way to sneak in a narration because everyone wants to tell something interesting.

So that's one example of a literature-based homeschooling day. Of course, yours may look completely different – we all want to see what other homeschool families are doing, assuming someone else has figured out the best way. True story, there is no such thing as a "best way" when it comes to homeschooling. Other people do what works best for their children, but you have to do what works the best for yours. But I think we're all pretty similar in the end, just parents doing our best to educate our children at home.

# Chapter 12 - The Art of Combining: Teaching Multiple Ages Together

Often when you think of homeschooling, you imagine the quintessential "one-room-school-house." This phrase conjures up images of a dining room table, a wall covered in maps and children's art. Two to four children sitting around the table, all studying at their own level, while a smiling mother patiently works her way around the table to each of her darling, quiet children.

The reality of a "one-room-schoolhouse" homeschool is both similar and yet very different. Those darling children are rarely quiet, and that dining room table can just as easily be a couch in the living room, a blanket in the backyard, or a mini-van as you run around town catching up on errands and taking children to outside activities. The demands on our time can make homeschooling multiple children seem intimidating, but it doesn't have to be!

I've often found that our easiest school years were those when everyone was studying the same historic period and the same science topic. It makes planning easier, we can do group projects, read the same books… it's just all around easier. My number one rule when it comes to staying sane while homeschooling is **Keep It Simple**. Whenever possible, I like to simplify. One of the best ways to streamline my day is to include all of my children in the same lessons whenever possible.

Obviously, you can't combine every subject – a 6 year old can't do the same level of math as a 12 year old. So certain subjects will need to be individualized. Mainly, these will be the foundational subjects, those that are built upon year after year, like math and language arts. However, the content subjects – history, geography, science, literature, art – these can be done as a family quite well.

Having flexible lesson plans is one of the keys to a "Keep It Simple" streamlined homeschool day. If your children are fairly close in age, it's easy to combine them in one time period or science topic. Great literature is still great literature, whether you are 7 or 77, so a wide age range can benefit from great read alouds, like *Charlotte's Web* or *Harry Potter and the Sorcerer's Stone*. One of my favorite quotes about children's literature is from C.S. Lewis:

> *"A children's story that can only be enjoyed by children is not a good children's story in the slightest."*

Good literature can and should be enjoyed by everyone in the family.

When you teach all of your children the same content subjects, you can still assign age-specific projects. For example, if you are studying ancient Egypt with a 7 year old, a 10 year old and a 14 year old, you would read your spine text and literature to everyone. Then you might assign your 7 year old to draw a picture of a sarcophagus, or narrate to you the steps in which mummies are made. Your 10 year old could learn about hieroglyphs and create a piece of artwork in the style of Ancient Egyptian art, incorporating what they've learned about hieroglyphs. Your 14 year old could write a biography about one of the pharaohs you've studied, or they could design a timeline of major events in Ancient Egyptian history.

Each of them could also have independent reading that ties into their history – *Tut's Mummy Lost and Found* (1988) by Judy Donnelly for your 7 year old, *A Place in the Sun* (1997) by Jill Rubalcaba for your 10 year old and *Tales of Ancient Egypt* (1967) by Roger Lancelyn Green for your 14 year old. In this way, everyone is studying the same general subject matter as a group, but then are able to delve deeper into that subject as appropriate for their age level.

But don't let yourself get too carried away with the idea of doing all of your subjects together. The art of combining your children together within content subjects is all about **keeping it simple**. There are so many fantastic options on the market today and tons of glossy catalogs full of shiny new curriculum.

It's hard to not want to include all of it! And if we're not careful, we overspend on curriculum, thinking we can fit it all into our day, and discover that we simply just cannot. I remember poring over all those catalogs when I first started homeschooling. The promise of the "perfect program" was a siren song to an excited newbie homeschooling mother. We all want the best for our children, but do they actually need all that stuff to become educated?

## *I don't need to cover everything every single year.*

Let that sink in… because it took me a while to let myself believe it. But it's true. You don't need to cover every single subject every year.

One of the things I adore about the Charlotte Mason style of education is that you can present your children with a wide array of beautiful ideas, with short lessons and in a way that connections are easily made. We don't need to spend hours studying grammar, and spelling, and handwriting, and reading comprehension, and vocabulary, and writing every year… We can cover those things through reading, narration, copywork and dictation. That doesn't mean that we never need to study grammar in depth – but you certainly don't need to every single year. We can let the literature, science, history and art blend together as one easily flows into the other. To me, this style of learning just makes sense.

One of the things I often hear from people, is that they aren't sure if they are doing enough. How does one define "enough?" When I look at a typical course of study for each grade level, it can be intimidating. There is just so much there! And when it comes to science and social studies especially, the subject matter can seem choppy and scattered. How can one teach all of those subjects within a cohesive framework? This type of homeschooling leads to a long list of items that must be checked off each day. It leads to tedious busy work and overwhelmed mothers trying to make sure they cover everything.

Rather, I look at the overall goal: what do I want to cover throughout the course of their entire homeschooling career? What do I want them to care about? What books do I want them to read? What is important to my individual child? There is no one size fits all when it comes to education! When you look at their education as a whole, everything makes more sense. The pieces ultimately and eventually all fit together, like a puzzle.

When you look at your individual child, you can see where you need to focus more and where you can relax and let things go. For example, my oldest daughter is a natural speller and a gifted writer. She hopes to become an author someday. She loves history and reading, but science doesn't interest her very much and math is her least favorite subject.

Grammar and spelling were never things we spent much time on, because she just seemed to naturally pick them up from all her reading. Because her goals lead to a focus on writing and literature, that is where I tend to put the most emphasis for her. She still has to cover math and science, but my goal there is to be sure we hit the basics and tick off the boxes we need to for college admissions. We don't need to stress ourselves out about advanced placement level sciences or calculus, because they aren't necessary for her and it would be torture to push her into it for the sake of beefing up her transcript.

My twins, on the other hand, are very different. They are musicians, and one is an artist. They are considering the possibilities of a music career, and neither are very academic. The bulk of their days are spent on music and art, so my goal for them is to still cover the basics, but give them plenty of space for creativity.

So what does a simplified Charlotte Mason style education look like?

Living books are the foundation – reading beautiful, well-written books can fill your child's mind with ideas, leading down rabbit trails into other subjects.

Reading a wide variety of great books will set the tone for your schooling. Your child will narrate what they read – first orally and eventually in writing, leading them to learn to craft essays and begin to analyze literature. They'll learn vocabulary in context and use passages from literature as copywork and later dictation.

You study history chronologically so that you can begin to see the flow of centuries and how one leads to another. Therefore, keeping a timeline is important. We aren't memorizing specific dates and names, but we are watching the pageant of time unfold before us. A timeline will help them to see the grand scope of time. We are finding out about the people that lived and how they changed our world. We are using well-written, real books to pin those facts to memory. You'll learn geography as it pertains to history, watching empires rise and fall and seeing how the maps change through the course of time. You'll get a glimpse of life in other cultures through beautiful stories and well-chosen documentaries and movies.

Art and literature can easily both tie into your history – you'll study the art work that came out of the turbulent times in which the artists lived, and read books that will allow you to "visit" those time periods. You can fit in classics, such as *To Kill a Mockingbird* (1960) by Harper Lee or *Adventures of Huckleberry Finn* (1884) by Mark Twain, while studying the time period in which they were written, to get a feel for how people spoke or thought during that time.

You might only focus on one or two science topics per year, digging in and exploring them with well written books, fascinating documentaries and some enlightening experiments.

This summer, we are planning our garden. I want to encourage my children to join in, so we're making it into a big family project. We're going to learn about composting and collecting rainwater, we'll test our soil and study what soil needs to grow the best veggies. We'll plan and plot our garden, learn about what bugs are good for the garden and which to avoid and study ways to keep those pests away without harming the environment and keep journals as we garden to learn what works and what doesn't. My teens will create time-lapse videos of a plant growing…all of this will flow very naturally. We have an end product – delicious produce that we cultivated ourselves. But even more, my children will be learning. They'll be studying botany and environmental science, but there will be no quizzes or tests or mindless busy work. Everything has a purpose.

With this type of schooling, you're using the best resources so although you aren't checking off endless boxes each day, you are still giving your children a powerful and thorough education. Each piece of the puzzle brings its value and worth to the table. There is no busy work to "get through." Your child's time is more important than that.

## But what about gaps?

Yes, there will be gaps. Everyone has gaps in their education. We can't know everything. That is an impossible goal. If you teach your child to read, and read well, and you show them how to seek out information, then any gaps they have will be easily filled in when the time comes. And when they need to find that information for themselves, when it's important to them, either because they are trying to apply for a competitive college, or because they are seeking employment, they will be able to pick up that information so much faster.

My twins were never interested in learning to type. It just wasn't something they cared to learn correctly. I would cringe whenever I saw them typing with two fingers, but they hated practicing the right way. This past year the amount of writing they need to do has increased greatly, and they wanted to increase their speed. Finally they had a reason to study typing! Now they are picking up the correct method, but they are doing it because it is important to them.

When you simplify – you give your child freedom. You can do your lessons in the morning and leave your afternoons open to explore, to play, or to daydream. You'll give your children time to try new things, time to just be. In this world of rush, rush, rush, it's a real gift to allow our children that space to breathe.

So yes, mothers, you are doing enough. You are giving your children a beautiful education, filled with ideas, and heroes, the poetry and lyricism of language and exploration of the world around them. You're giving them the freedom to imagine and explore. What could be more important than that?

# Chapter 13 - "An Atmosphere, a Discipline, a Life" Creating an Educational Environment

I used to daydream about creating a beautiful school room. I know you've all seen at least one gorgeous school room that was shared in an online forum, on a homeschool blog or Pinterest. They are amazing, right? Organized, bright and cheery, the perfect place to fill your children's mind with knowledge. Alas, my home is too small to allow a whole room devoted to our homeschooling.

Charlotte Mason says that "education is an atmosphere, a discipline, a life." To me, that says that our schooling doesn't need to be contained to one room in our house. I want our whole lives to be our "school" – not just one room where I can hide our ongoing projects and books. She's also saying that there is more to it than just providing an inspiring space in our homes. Everything we do, our entire lives, can either inspire or hinder our children's education.

There are three keys to creating an educational environment in your home: **surroundings**, **routine**, and **relationships**. When these three things are in order, your home, whether it has space for one of those gorgeous school rooms or not, will be the perfect learning environment for your children. Let's begin though with the most prominent aspect of creating an educational and literary atmosphere – our home surroundings.

## Surroundings

When you homeschool with a living books philosophy, you're going to need to invest in building a good home library. But if you're like me, you're probably on a pretty tight budget. Being a literary homeschooler doesn't mean you have to spend a small fortune or go into debt providing your children with an expansive home library. I've been an avid book collector for as long as I can remember, but I'm also extremely careful with our money. Some might even say that I'm cheap.

I think it's important to set boundaries about which books you are going to include in your home library. Otherwise, you'll end up buying everything. The first thing I always check is to see what my local public library carries. If I can borrow it for free, then I probably don't need to purchase it. My little town library is always my first stop when we need to research a particular subject or just want something new to read.

To me, visiting the library is a great way to spend an afternoon. Libraries are often an overlooked source of fantastic material, from books and magazines to museum passes and free foreign language study materials. Yes, you need to be careful that you don't run up any fines. I keep all of our library books in a basket in our living room. I've taught my children to always return their library books to said basket when they have finished reading them. It took some time (and a lot of reminding), but we rarely have any overdue books. My library actually saves us money!

I do sometimes purchase a book for our home library that we can find at our town library. These are the books that I find my children choosing over and over again. If a book I'm looking for isn't available locally at my library or through their extensive inter-library loan network, then I'll buy it. But I rarely run out to the big fancy chain bookstore. Being the bargain hunter that I am, I refuse to spend a small fortune on a book. So how can you still provide your family with a great home library without breaking the bank?

My favorite ways to get great books for very little money are to hit the used book sales. Check your local library (and neighboring libraries) for sales –

mine has a porch sale every spring, and the big city library 15 minutes away has a huge sale around the same time. I can get stacks of books for just a few dollars. You can check the Book Sale Finder website (http://booksalefinder.com) to see what sales are in your area.

Amazon.com is great for shopping for books on a budget. If you pay attention, they have sales all the time and you can get some great deals. For example – the 11 book *History of US* set is a fabulous resource, but it can often be pricey. These books are fantastic – they are colorful and well written, making history come alive. I especially appreciate that her books are more about the people who made history rather than memorizing a bunch of dates and names. She makes George Washington, Abraham Lincoln, Harriet Tubman, and Franklin D. Roosevelt feel like real people, who had to make real choices, rather than just facts to be remembered.

But these books, fantastic as they are, can cost a fortune if you aren't careful. Retail value is $175! But every now and then, Amazon will drop the price for a day or two. A few years ago, I purchased the set brand new for around $89. But when you see a great deal like this you need to act fast, as prices can change overnight. There are sites like Book Outlet (bookoutlet.com), Thrift Books (thriftbooks.com), and Overstock (overstock.com) that specialize in selling discounted books. They don't have everything and their inventory is always changing, but it's a great place to check frequently when you are looking for a specific title.

Thrift shops can also be a great way to get a great deal on books – I love book-hunting at Goodwill. I've gotten some gorgeous books for extremely cheap. Along the same lines, you can find great deals at yard sales and flea markets as well. You might even be surprised at what you can find for cheap on eBay.

The most important thing though – know what you are looking for. Even with great deals, you can end up spending too much on things you didn't necessarily need. My house is small, so unfortunately shelf space is limited. I can't tell you how many times I've had to purge books to make space – it's not easy! But if a book hasn't left the shelf for over a year and I won't need it in the near future, it might have to go. To keep from making too many spontaneous purchases, I keep a list in my purse of all the books I'm currently looking for. I try to shop at least one school year ahead. This helps me to avoid purchases of books I don't need, no matter how pretty or cool or fun they might look. I mean, how many dinosaur books does one family need anyway? (Because we have over 50... seriously.)

But there are other items besides books you'll want to have in your home to inspire learning. I highly recommend you keep a big world map in a prominent place in your home. You will be amazed at how much geographic knowledge your children pick up just by looking over the map (when it's at eye level in a prominent place, I promise they'll look at it frequently), finding the places you read about in your daily read aloud, looking up places you hear about on the news or on television.

Casual geography lessons are often the best way to ensure your child won't end up on one of those embarrassing "man on the street" interviews where some poor shmoe points to Canada when asked to locate India on a map. It will also make them much more aware of current events when they are older – a teen/adult who has a working knowledge of basic geography will be able to comprehend news about the Middle East or famine in Africa. We need to ensure that our children are geographically literate in our increasingly global society.

When my children were smaller, they created a game where someone would call out the name of a country and they would race to see who could find it first. This often led to wondering about who lives in those strange-sounding places, which often led to finding a book or movie about said country. Everything is connected in this style of education, and it's all about making those connections!

Another must for your learning environment is a place to store nature finds. I like to have a shelf in our living room dedicated to this. When my children discover a rock or wildflower, or a small nest with the empty egg shell (check your local laws – it can be illegal in some places to remove a nest), or a handful of acorns, we display them on our nature shelf. This legitimizes your child's discoveries, and gives you a chance to look up their treasures in a field guide. I'll often arrange them artistically, giving them something to draw in their journals before we have to clear the shelf for the next find.

If you have the wall space, you can display some art in your home. You can find art prints for fairly cheap online, and then frame them with an inexpensive frame. If you don't have the wall space, another great way to display art is to find those gorgeous coffee table type art books, which are generally full of full color art prints. You can set this out with a cookbook stand, or just open on the table, for perusing. Change out the art every couple of months to give your children exposure to a variety of artists and styles.

Do you find that science doesn't happen as much as you would like? Strew some interesting books around and have a few fun science kits on hand and out where your child can easily spot them and I guarantee they will want to pick them up. Leave a pair of binoculars in a window where there are trees nearby and let your child watch for birds. Set up a telescope in a window and look at the stars and planets. Put together a "nature study bag" with a magnifying glass, small baggies, a pencil and nature notebook, and small jars for collecting bugs, and be sure to bring it with you when you play outside. Just being prepared and having plenty of interesting materials on hand will inspire you and your child to explore and learn.

Inspiring a love of learning in our children is one of the most important things we can do. Fill your home with the best-of-the-best children's literature and art, but don't break the bank doing it. With some careful shopping, you can provide your child with a great home library where they can learn and dream and grow.

Most of all though, you want to be sure that your home is at least somewhat organized and tidy. It is far easier for our children to concentrate on their studies when their environment is clean and not chaotic, and everything has a place.

## Routine

Another aspect of having an educational atmosphere is to keep to a routine. This is not the same as a schedule. I don't know about you, but schedules don't go over well in my household. I once created an elaborate schedule, down to the minute, for myself and all of my children. It was perfect and would keep all of us on task, giving us plenty of time to complete our school work, chores and outside activities. Unfortunately, unless we were slaves to a clock, it was impossible to follow. Instead, I created a routine, or a rhythm for our day. Rather than tracking our day by the minute, I created a set of activities that we needed to do each day. It looked something like this:

**Morning Routine:**

- o Wake/Shower/Dress
- o Make Breakfast
- o Morning Basket (read aloud, geography, poetry)
- o Clean kitchen and start laundry

**Late Morning Routine:**

- o Twins – math and music practice (alternate)
- o School time with Regina
- o Dictation and Writing with the twins
- o Snack Break and once a week nature walk
- o Art lesson/project
- o Quiet Reading time (Check in with Sarah, go over assignments)

**Afternoon Routine:**

- o Lunch (read aloud literature)
- o Geography and Science (Sarah piano practice)
- o Twins music practice
- o Afternoon chores

**Late Afternoon Routine:**

- Computer check in, work time for Mom, free time for kids
- Outdoor play (weather permitting)

**Evening Routine:**

- Make dinner (Check in with Dad about our day)
- Once a week game night/movie night

This gives our day a structure without having to constantly check the clock to be sure we have time to get it all done. By hinging things to just morning or late morning, it opens up our time. We can get started at 7am if we're up, but if we had a late night and we all sleep until 9, it won't mean that our day is ruined. We'll just jump in and adjust as we go. This is a typical at home day. If we had activities or errands to run, we'd do those in the afternoon after our academics were finished.

I try to always keep to our morning routine. This ensures that we don't get behind in the 3R's or that we must squeeze them into the evenings. Remember too that Charlotte Mason recommended short lessons.

Even when you have a full schedule of lessons planned they won't take the entire day to complete. A six-year-old should only be spending 10 – 20 minutes on any one subject. Even a high schooler needn't spend more than 45 minutes on any subject.

Having a plan makes life easier, so meal planning is a must. I don't claim to be an expert here, but when I take the time to plan our meals for the week it eliminates a quite a bit of stress. I can share what I do, and hopefully it will inspire you to get organized and plan your meals.

I suggest keeping a short list of favorite simple breakfast and lunch meals, like bagels, scrambled eggs and bacon, oatmeal, grilled cheese, PB&J, soup, etc. and rotating through them so you aren't eating the same meals every single day. Try to keep the necessary ingredients on hand. Having a well-stocked pantry makes meal planning easy. I don't do anything elaborate for those meals during the week. "Keep it simple" is my mantra. On days when things get crazy, or mom is sick, my kids can handle their own meals because everything is near to hand and easy to make.

The main focus for me when it comes to meal planning is dinner. This is the meal that gives me the most stress. If I don't plan ahead, I start panicking around 4pm…what will we eat? What do I have that I can throw together? Can I get away with serving frozen waffles? I try to stay one step ahead by planning for a week in advance. Saturday mornings, I go through my kitchen and make a menu for the week. I try to incorporate ingredients that I already have on hand and then I add anything I still need to my grocery list. I try to keep a well-stocked pantry, with plenty of sauces, pastas, rice, veggies, and seasonings, so that meal planning is easy. I should always have enough on hand to fix at least 2-3 staple meals. I call these my emergency meals, as they are the ones I can fix at the last minute when the day has been hectic.

I try to get the family involved and let them weigh in on what they'd like to eat for the week, and sometimes they'll request their favorites. When I'm sick of everything we've been eating, I head to Pinterest and look for new and different recipes. But often I just try to keep to a simple rotation. We have several meals that are staples; spaghetti and meatballs, Asian style tuna cakes with rice and broccoli, and tacos (or taco salad) Then I have more open-ended meals like a chicken dish, a meatless meal, and a fun meal (pizza, breakfast for dinner, make-at-home take-out).

Once I've pulled together my menu for the week, I finish writing the grocery list and post the menu on the refrigerator where everyone can see it. The idea is to keep the kids from constantly asking me what we're having for dinner...alas, they can't seem to resist that question. It also helps me to pay attention and pull out frozen meat the night before so it will be ready to cook the next day.

Another tip is to know your schedule! If I know I'm going to have an exceptionally busy day, I'll plan a slow cooker meal for that day so I won't have to worry about dinner. Running around all day and then having to come home and fix a big meal is a recipe for burn out! Give yourself a break on those days and start dinner in the morning so that when you come home, you can just serve up dinner and relax.

Pinterest is a wealth of information when it comes to meal planning and recipes. I also like the site allrecipes.com, because the recipes have reviews. I like to know before I try something new if a recipe is worth making.

Having a plan eliminates so much stress. So take the time to plan your meals and save yourself time and aggravation.

## Relationships

When children bicker all day, and mom is constantly checking her phone or laptop, the home is not a peaceful place conducive to learning. Keeping to a routine will help, but if there is still contention in the ranks, your home will not run smoothly.

I think that it is of the utmost importance to encourage sibling friendships. This can be difficult if you have a wide age range, but even then, if you can encourage your older child to befriend their younger sibling, it will go a long way to create a happy home environment. This can be challenging when we are always home and always together. I try very hard to give my children enough space to have time alone if they need it, and I'll admit to using the bathroom as a sanctuary to have 10 minutes of peaceful time alone when it is absolutely necessary.

Teaching our children about boundaries will go a long way to instilling a peaceful learning environment in your home. We have very strict rules about no hitting and being respectful of other people's things. Learning these things at home when they are young will help our children grow into responsible and respectful adults.

Another thing I want very much to instill in my children is that sibling bonds are forever. I want them to all be able to get along as adults, so I encourage friendships now. Part of that bond is through engaging them in family read alouds and studying the same subjects together as a family. But we also do fun things like family movie nights, board game nights, field trips and excursions to interesting places around town, and fun family days where we play Pokémon Go or have a picnic at the local park. These times together aren't fancy, nor do they require much planning, but they do wonders to increase our family bond and grow sibling friendships. That's not to say they never argue, but they have never had a spat that lasted more than an afternoon.

I also expect that my children will help with housework. We all live here, so we all contribute. When mom (or dad) has to do all of the housework and everyone else just adds to the workload, this does not make for a parent who is able to peacefully teach their children. Resentment can be an ugly thing. Spend some time teaching your children to properly do some of the housework so that you do not have such a heavy burden to bear. Being the parent AND the teacher is difficult enough without adding full time chef and housekeeper on top of it.

A six-year-old can put away their laundry and clean off the table after meals. A 10-year-old can run the vacuum and dust. A teenager can run the dishwasher and do laundry. All of them are expected to keep their rooms neat and tidy. Everyone can help to keep their environment neat and organized, which makes for a much less stressful home. It is so much easier to focus on lessons and reading those wonderful books when you don't have laundry piled up to your eyeballs and a sink full of dirty dishes.

When I reflect on the words, "Education is an atmosphere, a discipline, a life," I like to think that I'm giving my children the best possible environment to learn and grow. By giving thought to their surroundings, giving them meaningful work and beautiful ideas to think about, by teaching them to be helpful contributors to the household, I am ensuring that they will be helpful contributors to the world. I'm raising them not just to be intelligent and well read, but good communicators, people who care about the environment and have empathy towards others. I wholeheartedly believe that when we give our children the space to learn and grow, real learning can and will happen.

# Afterward: A Love Letter to my Children

A love letter to my children:

One of the best things I ever did was read aloud to
you. From the time you were small, in some cases in
the womb, you listened to me read story after story.
We joined in the wild rumpus with Max and the Wild
Things, quickly ate a strawberry with a little mouse to
keep it from the hungry bear, and climbed the
coconut tree with the alphabet.

We learned about heroes like George Washington and
Squanto, and villains like Dolores Umbridge and
General Woundwort. You learned about friendship,
death, courage, and bravery, all at my knee. We spent
long days immersed in birding, the solar system, or
Elizabethan England, just exploring.

I look back on our homeschool days – they seemed so
long and tiresome some days. But overall, it's been all
too short. Someday, very soon, you will go out into
the world on your own. I have given you a gift. The
stories I shared with you, they aren't just words on
paper. They are life – lives lived by characters in the
imagination, but lived nonetheless.

When you see someone who needs help – I hope you
remember Charlotte and Wilbur. When life is hard
and everything seems to be falling apart, remember

Sara Crewe and find a way to change your outlook. When you feel that something is wrong but everyone is ignoring you, remember Hazel and Fiver and persevere. They've all shown you a way ahead.

Books aren't just for school. They are for life, for living your best life and seeing the world from the safety of your home. They are there when you want to take risks and explore, and when things are hard and you just want to hide. When you are homesick, I hope you will find a piece of home in the stories we read. I'll be there, between those pages – reading the story in the quiet of your mind.

I hope that someday, when you have children of your own, you'll remember those moments and how special they were, and you'll share your favorites with them. It's a gift, so pass it on.


Love, Mama

# Appendix: Favorite Books by Grade Level

This list is by no means meant to be a definitive book list. Book lists are subjective, and these are books that I personally have loved or that my children have loved. I believe they are worthy of being read and they all fall under the category of "living books" but there are many other fantastic books that aren't on this list. I tried to include a range of genres and subject matter, from literature and poetry, to science and history.

Many of the books on the list are by authors who I think it is worth your time to explore. So, for example, if you enjoy *The Little House* by Virginia Lee Burton, you might also want to look for *Mike Mulligan and His Steam Shovel*, or *Katy and the Big Snow*.

I am dividing this list into age range categories, but many of the books can be enjoyed by children younger and older – as C.S. Lewis once said:

> *"No book is really worth reading at the age of ten which is not equally – and often far more – worth reading at the age of fifty and beyond."*

I've labeled the book list for ease of use:

S/M = Science or Math          G = Geography
P = Poetry                     H = History

# Ages 3 - 6

*Caps for Sale* Esphyr Slobodkina
*Why Mosquitoes Buzz in People's Ears* - Verna Aardema (G)
*The Little House* - Virginia Lee Burton
*Life Story* - Virginia Lee Burton
*The Knight and the Dragon* - Tomie dePaola (H)
*The Art Lesson* - Tomie dePaola
*Strega Nona* - Tomie dePaola
*Where the Wild Things Are* - Maurice Sendak
*A Pair of Red Clogs* - Masako Matsuno
*We Are In a Book!* - Mo Willems
*Ferdinand* - Munro Leaf (G)
*The Three Snow Bears* - Jan Brett
*The Mitten* - Jan Brett
*The Umbrella* - Jan Brett
*How Much is a Million?* - David M. Schwartz (M)
*The Snowy Day* - Ezra Jack Keats
*Chicka Chicka Boom Boom* - Bill Martin Jr.
*The Little Mouse, The Red Ripe Strawberry, And the Big Hungry Bear* - Don Wood
*Owl Moon* - Jane Yolen (S)
*Owl Babies* - Martin Waddell (S)
*Blueberries for Sal* - Robert McClosky
*Water is Water* - Miranda Paul (S)
*I Love You Stinky Face* - Lisa McCourt
*The Day the Crayons Came Home* - Drew Daywalt
*Tales of Peter Rabbit* - Beatrix Potter
*I, Crocodile* - Fred Marcellino
*The Seven Chinese Sisters* - Kathy Tucker
*I Am Jane Goodall* - Brad Meltzer (S)

*Our Family Tree: An Evolution Story*– Lisa Westberg Peters (S)

*Grandmother Fish* – Jonathan Tweet (S)

*The Book with No Pictures* – B.J. Novak

*Toot and Puddle* – Holly Hobbie

*Jambo Means Hello* – Muriel and Tom Feelings (G)

*Marvin K Mooney Will You Please Go Now!* – Dr. Suess

*My Name is Yoon* – Helen Recorvits (G)

*Just Go to Bed* – Mercer Mayer

*The Monster at the End of This Book* – Jon Stone

*How Pizza Came to Queens* – Dayal Kaur Khalsa (G)

*Planting the Wild Garden* – Kathryn O. Galbraith (S)

*On a Beam of Light: A Story of Albert Einstein* – Jennifer Berne (S)

*Read Aloud Rhymes for the Very Young* – Jack Prelutsky (P)

*A Seed is Sleepy* – Diana Aston and Sylvia Long (S)

*Snowflake Bentley* – Jacqueline Briggs Martin (S)

*A Weed is a Flower: The Life of George Washington Carver* – Aliki (S)

*A Medieval Feast* – Aliki (H)

## Ages 7 – 9

*The Tale of Despereaux* – Kate DiCamillo
*Little Pear* – Eleanor Frances Lattimore (G/H)
*Ramona the Pest* – Beverly Cleary
*The Mouse and the Motorcycle* – Beverly Cleary
*See Saw Girl* – Linda Sue Park (G/H)
*The BFG* – Roald Dahl
*Matilda* – Roald Dahl
*My Father's Dragon* – Ruth Stiles Gannett
*The Prairie Thief* – Melissa Wiley
*Castle Diary* – Richard Platt (H)
*Shakespeare Stories* – Leon Garfield
*A Treasury of Children's Literature* – Armand Eisen
*Coral Reefs* – Jason Chin (S)
*Hanna, Homeschooler* – Suki Wessling
*Dear America: A Journey to the New World* – Kathryn Lasky (H)
*Winnie the Pooh* – A.A. Milne
*Pippi Longstocking* – Astrid Lindgren
*Where the Sidewalk Ends* – Shel Silverstein (P)
*Bunnicula* – James Howe
*The Invention of Hugo Cabret* – Brian Selznick
*Summer Birds: The Butterflies of Maria Merian* – Margarita Engle (S)
*The Cricket in Times Square* – George Selden
*One Beetle Too Many: The Extraordinary Adventures of Charles Darwin* – Kathryn Lasky (S/H)
*Magic School Bus: Inside the Human Body* – Joanna Cole (S)
*If You Decide to Go to the Moon* – Faith McNulty (S)
*Ben and Me* – Robert Lawson (H)
*Molly's Pilgrim* – Barbara Cohen (H/G)

*Mercy Watson to the Rescue* – Kate DiCamillo

*Why is Art Full of Naked People? And Other Vital Questions About Art* – Susie Hodge

*Vincent's Starry Night and Other Stories: A Child's History of Art* – Michael Bird

*One Small Square: Seashore* – Donald Silver (S)

*Girls Who Looked Under Rocks* – Jeannine Atkins (S)

*The Birchbark House* – Louise Erdrich (H)

*Sarah, Plain and Tall* – Patricia MacLachlan

*Animalium* – Jenny Broom (S)

*If: A Mind-bending New Way of Looking At Big Ideas nad Numbers* – David J. Smith (S/M)

*Classic Treasury of Aesop's Fables* – Don Daily

*Nelson Mandela's Favorite African Folktales* – Nelson Mandela (G)

*Math Fables* – Greg Tang (M)

*Nature Anatomy* – Julia Rothman (S)

*George's Secret Key to the Universe* – Lucy and Stephen Hawking (S)

*Under the Weather: Stories About Climate Change* – Tony Bradman (S)

*Where the Mountain Meets the Moon* – Grace Lin (G)

*Shanleya's Quest: A Botany Adventure for Kids Age 9 – 99* – Thomas J. Elpel (S)

*The Hundred Dresses* – Eleanor Estes

*Sky Tree: Seeing Science Through Art* – Thomas Locker (S)

*Zoey and Sassafras series* – Asia Citro (S)

*Knock at a Star: A Child's Introduction to Poetry* – X.J. Kennedy (P)

# Ages 10 - 13

*Mistakes that Worked* – Charlotte Jones (S/H)
*Harry Potter and the Sorcerer's Stone* – J.K. Rowling
*A Wrinkle in Time* – Madeleine L'Engle
*The Sherwood Ring* – Elizabeth Marie Pope
*The Mysterious Benedict Society* – Trenton Lee Stewart
*The Hobbit* – J.R.R. Tolkien
*Rules* – Cynthia Lord
*The War That Saved My Life* – Kimberly Brubaker Bradley (H)
*Shooting Kabul* – N.H. Senzai (G/H)
*Book Scavenger* – Jennifer Chambliss Bertman
*The Magic of Reality* – Richard Dawkins (S)
*Anna of Byzantium* – Tracy Barrett (H)
*Inside Out and Back Again* – Thanhha Lai (G/H)
*The Apprentice* – Pilar Molina Llorente (H)
Poetry for Young People series (P)
*Because of Winn Dixie* – Kate DiCamillo
*Gregor the Overlander* – Suzanne Collins
*D'Aulaire's Greek Mythology* – Ingri and Edgar Parin D'Aulaire
*Mrs. Frisby and the Rats of NIMH* – Robert C. O'Brien
*The Phantom Tollbooth* – Norton Juster
*Evolution of Calpurnia Tate* – Jacqueline Kelly
*One Crazy Summer* – Rita Williams-Garcia
*Phineas Gage: A Gruesome but True Story About Brain Science* – John Fleischman (S)
*The Number Devil: A Mathematical Adventure* – Hans Magnus Enzensberger (M)
*Journey to Jo-Burg: A South African Story* – Beverley Naidoo (G/H)

*Rad Women Worldwide* – Kate Schatz (G/H/S)
*A Little Piece of Ground* – Elizabeth Laird (H/G)
*Along Came Galileo* – Jeanne Bendick (H/S)
*Pagoo* – Holling C. Holling (S)
*The Story of Clocks and Calendars* – Betsy Maestro (S/M/H)
*The One and Only Ivan* – Katherine Applegate
*Frindle* – Andrew Clements
*Anne of Green Gables* – L.M. Montgomery
*Wonder* – R.J. Palacio
*When You Reach Me* – Rebecca Stead
*Tuck Everlasting* – Natalie Babbitt
*Bone: Out from Boneville* – Jeff Smith
*The Giver* – Lois Lowery
*The Wollstonecraft Detective Agency: The Case of the Missing Moonstone* – Jordan Stratford
*Find the Constellations* – H.A. Rey (S)
*The Way Things Work* – David Macaulay (S)
*Weather!* – Rebecca Rupp (S)
*The Graveyard Book* – Neil Gaiman
*From the Mixed-Up Files of Mrs. Basil E. Frankweiler* – E.L. Konigsberg
*Chains* – Laurie Halse Anderson
*A Midsummer Night's Dream* – William Shakespeare
*Macbeth* – William Shakespeare
*Breaking Stalin's Nose* – Eugene Yelchin (G/H)
*Shadow Spinner* – Susan Fletcher

# Ages 14+

*The Hunger Games trilogy* – Suzanne Collin
*Lord of the Rings* – J.R.R. Tolkein
*The Book Thief* – Markus Zuzak  (H)
*Mary, Bloody Mary* – Carolyn Meyer (H)
*A Short History of Nearly Everything* – Bill Bryson (S)
*Nation* – Terry Pratchett
*Adventures of Huckleberry Finn* – Mark Twain
*Eva* – Peter Dickinson
*Great Expectations* – Charles Dickens
*American Born Chinese* – Gene Luen Yang (G)
*Climate Changed: A Personal Journey Through Science* –
Philippe Squarzoni (S)
*Kindred* – Octavia E. Butler (H)
*A Book of Luminous Things: An International Anthology of
Poetry* – Czeslaw Milosz (P)
*The Sixth Extinction* – Elizabeth Kolbert (S)
*Material World: A Global Family Portrait* – Peter Menzel (G)
*Watership Down* – Richard Adams
*The Song of Achilles* – Madeline Miller
*Salt: A World History* – Mark Kurlansky  (H)
*Jane Eyre* – Charlotte Bronte
*Things Fall Apart* – Chinua Achebe
*The Great Gatsby* – F. Scott Fitzgerald
*To Kill a Mockingbird* – Harper Lee
*1984* – George Orwell
*Animal Farm* – George Orwell

*The Demon-Haunted World: Science as a Candle in the Dark* –
Carl Sagan (S)
*Hamlet* – William Shakespeare
*Much Ado About Nothing* – William Shakespeare
*The Handmaid's Tale* – Margaret Atwood
*Night* – Elie Wiesel (H)
*Of Mice and Men* – John Steinbeck
*Flowers for Algernon* – Daniel Keyes
*Wolf by Wolf* – Ryan Graudin
*The Hitchhiker's Guide to the Galaxy* – Douglas Adams
*The Complete Persopolis* – Marjane Satrapi (G)
*Every Day* – David Levithan
*The Absolutely True Diary of a Part-Time Indian* – Sherman
Alexie
*Red Scarf Girl: A Memoir of the Cultural Revolution* – Ji-li
Jiang (G/H)
*I Am Malala* – Malala Yousafzai (G)
*Bomb* – Steve Sheinkin (S/H)
*The Good Earth* – Pearl S. Buck
*The Immortal Life of Henrietta Lacks* – Rebecca Skloot (S/H)
*Farewell to Manzanar* – Jeanne Houston (H)
*Parallel Journeys* – Eleanor H. Ayer (H)
*100 Best-Loved Poems* – Philip Smith (P)
*Poetry 180* – Billy Collins (P)
*An Ember in the Ashes* – Sabaa Tahir
*Enchantress of the Stars* – Sylvia Engdahl
*Unwind* – Neal Shusterman

## Resources for learning more about Charlotte Mason:

The Charlotte Mason Digital Collection at Redeemer College

https://www.redeemer.ca/academics/library/charlotte-mason-digitalcollection
https://archive.org/details/charlottemasondigitalcollection

You can find everything here, from her writings and theory to Parents' Review articles and explanations of how her methods were originally implemented.

# About the Author

**Emily Cook** is the author and creator of the secular homeschool curriculum Build Your Library, a literature-based K-10 program infused with the teachings of Charlotte Mason. She writes full year lesson plans as well as shorter topical unit studies.

Emily has been homeschooling her four children in Southern NH for over 14 years. She is passionate about reading aloud to children of all ages and loves to share her love of literature with others. She and her family also makes incredibly dorky videos about homeschooling, books and more on Youtube at ARRRGH! Schooling. You can follow her on Twitter, Pinterest and Facebook.

**http://BuildYourLibrary.com**

http://YouTube.com/ArrrghSchooling
http://Twitter.com/BYLibrary
http://Pinterest.com/BYLibrary
http://Facebook.com/BuildYourLibrary
http://feeds.Feedburner.com/BuildYourLibrary

Printed in Poland
by Amazon Fulfillment
Poland Sp. z o.o., Wrocław